CENTER
STREET

**LARGE
PRINT**

Books by Dr. John C. Maxwell
Can Teach You How to Be a REAL Success

Relationships

25 Ways to Win with People

Becoming a Person of Influence

Encouragement Changes Everything

Ethics 101

Everyone Communicates, Few Connect

The Power of Partnership

Relationships 101

Winning with People

Leadership

*The 10th Anniversary Edition of The 21
Irrefutable Laws of Leadership*

The 21 Indispensable Qualities of a Leader

*The 21 Most Powerful Minutes
in a Leader's Day*

The 360 Degree Leader

Developing the Leader Within You

The 5 Levels of Leadership

Go For Gold

Leadership 101

Leadership Gold

Leadership Promises for Every Day

Attitude

Attitude 101

The Difference Maker

Failing Forward

How Successful People Think

Success 101

Thinking for a Change

The Winning Attitude

Equipping

The 15 Invaluable Laws of Growth

*The 17 Essential Qualities of
a Team Player*

The 17 Indisputable Laws of Teamwork

Developing the Leaders Around You

Equipping 101

Make Today Count

Mentoring 101

My Dream Map

Partners in Prayer

Put Your Dream to the Test

Running with the Giants

Talent Is Never Enough

Today Matters

Your Road Map for Success

THE
15
INVALUABLE LAWS
—OF—
GROWTH

LIVE THEM AND
REACH YOUR POTENTIAL

JOHN C. MAXWELL

CENTER STREET

LARGE ■ PRINT

The author is represented by Yates & Yates, LLP,
Literary Agency, Orange, California.

Center Street
Hachette Book Group
237 Park Avenue
New York, NY 10017

www.centerstreet.com

Printed in the United States of America

RRD-C

First Edition: October 2012

10   9   8   7   6   5   4   3   2   1

Center Street is a division of Hachette Book Group, Inc.
The Center Street name and logo are trademarks of
Hachette Book Group, Inc.

The publisher is not responsible for websites (or their content)
that are not owned by the publisher.

Library of Congress Cataloging-in-Publication Data
Maxwell, John C., 1947–
The 15 invaluable laws of growth : live them and reach
your potential / John C. Maxwell.
        p. cm.
Includes bibliographical references.
ISBN 978-1-59995-366-3 (hardcover)—ISBN 978-1-4555-2285-9
(large print)
1. Self-actualization (Psychology)   2. Self-consciousness (Awareness)
3. Self-perception.   I. Title.   II. Title: Fifteen invaluable laws of growth.
BF637.S4M386 2012
158—dc23
2012012482

This book is dedicated to

The team at the John Maxwell Company:
You fulfill my vision,
you extend my influence, and
you make me better than I am.
Your work is helping others to maximize their
potential and impact their world.

And to Curt Kampmeier:
who introduced me to the concept of intentional
personal growth and in doing so
showed me the path to reaching my potential.

Contents

Acknowledgments   xi

Introduction   xiii

1. **The Law of Intentionality:** Growth
   Doesn't Just Happen   1

2. **The Law of Awareness:** You Must Know
   Yourself to Grow Yourself   23

3. **The Law of the Mirror:** You Must See
   Value *in* Yourself to Add Value *to* Yourself   51

4. **The Law of Reflection:** Learning to Pause
   Allows Growth to Catch Up with You   74

5. **The Law of Consistency:** Motivation
   Gets You Going—Discipline Keeps
   You Growing   99

6. **The Law of Environment:** Growth Thrives
   in Conducive Surroundings   122

7. **The Law of Design:** To Maximize Growth, Develop Strategies   147

8. **The Law of Pain:** Good Management of Bad Experiences Leads to Great Growth   178

9. **The Law of the Ladder:** Character Growth Determines the Height of Your Personal Growth   203

10. **The Law of the Rubber Band:** Growth Stops When You Lose the Tension Between Where You Are and Where You Could Be   229

11. **The Law of Trade-Offs:** You Have to Give Up to Grow Up   254

12. **The Law of Curiosity:** Growth Is Stimulated by Asking *Why?*   283

13. **The Law of Modeling:** It's Hard to Improve When You Have No One but Yourself to Follow   307

14. **The Law of Expansion:** Growth Always Increases Your Capacity   330

15. **The Law of Contribution:** Growing Yourself Enables You to Grow Others   355

Notes   383

Acknowledgments

Thank you to:
Charlie Wetzel, my writer;
Stephanie Wetzel, my social media manager;
Linda Eggers, my executive assistant.

Introduction

Potential is one of the most wonderful words in any language. It looks forward with optimism. It is filled with hope. It promises success. It implies fulfillment. It hints at greatness. Potential is a word based on possibilities. Think about your potential as a human being and you get excited—at least, I hope you do. What a positive thought. I believe in your potential just as much as I believe in mine. Do you have potential? Absolutely.

What about *unfulfilled potential*? That phrase is as negative as the word *potential* is positive. My friend Florence Littauer, a speaker and author, wrote a story in her book *Silver Boxes* about her father, who always wanted to be a singer but never was. She says he died with the music still inside of him. That's an apt description of unfulfilled potential. Not reaching your potential is like dying with the music still inside of you.

Since you are reading these words, I believe you

have the desire to reach your potential. So the question becomes, how do you do it?

I have no doubt that the answer is growth. To reach your potential you must grow. And to grow, you must be highly intentional about it. This book is my effort to help you learn how to grow and develop yourself so you have the best chance of becoming the person you were created to be. My desire is to help you develop the right attitude, learn more about your strengths, tap into your passion, become more in touch with your purpose, and develop your skills so you can be all you can be.

You may be aware that this is the third Laws book I've written. The first was developed to help leaders understand how leadership works so they could become better leaders. The second was to help people understand teamwork and develop stronger teams. This book is dedicated to helping you understand how personal growth works and to help you become a more effective and fulfilled individual. While it's true that I may include a few leadership insights along the way, you don't need to be a leader for this book to help you. You don't need to be part of a team to grow (though it certainly helps). You just need to be a person who wants to grow and become better than you are today.

What do I mean when I write about growth? That

will be as unique as you are. To discover your purpose, you need to grow in self-awareness. To become a better human being, you need to grow in character. To advance in your career, you need to grow in your skills. To be a better spouse or parent, you need to grow in relationships. To reach your financial goals, you need to grow in your knowledge about how money works. To enrich your soul, you need to grow spiritually. The specifics of growth change from person to person, but the principles are the same for every person. This book offers laws that will teach you how to approach the worthy goal of growing. It is a key that unlocks the door. You will have to put in the work to actually grow.

My recommendation is that you tackle a chapter of this book every week. Discuss it with some friends. Do the application exercises that are at the end of each chapter. Keep a growth journal. And incorporate what you're learning into your everyday life. You cannot change your life until you change something you do every day. By learning the laws and then living them, you will be on your way to reaching your potential. If you keep learning and growing every day over the course of many years, you will be astounded by how far it will take you.

1

The Law of Intentionality
Growth Doesn't Just Happen

Life is now in session. Are you present?

D o you have a plan for your personal growth?" Curt
Kampmeier, the man who asked me the question,
waited patiently for my response. It was a question
that would change my life.

I fumbled for answers. I listed my accomplishments from the previous three years. I talked about
how hard I worked. I outlined my goals. I explained
the things I was doing to reach more people. All of
my answers were based on activity, not on improving.
Finally I had to admit it. I had no plan to become
better.

It was something I had never considered before,
and it exposed a major flaw in my approach to work

and success. When I started my career, I was intentional about working, reaching my goals, and being successful. I had a strategy: hard work. I hoped that would get me where I wanted to go. But working hard doesn't guarantee success. And hope isn't a strategy.

How do you get better at what you do? How do you improve your relationships? How do you gain more depth and wisdom as a person? How do you gain insight? How do you overcome obstacles? Work harder? Work longer? Wait for things to get better?

That conversation happened over lunch at a Holiday Inn restaurant in 1972. At the time, I had just been given the opportunity to move up in my career. I had been offered the best church in my denomination. Think about being offered the top leadership job in the premier location in your company. That's what it was for me. The problem was that I was twenty-four years old, I was in way over my head, and I knew that if I didn't rise to the occasion, I would fail spectacularly.

Curt was a salesman who was selling a growth kit—a year-long plan with materials designed to help a person grow. He slid the brochure across the table to me. It cost $799, which was nearly a month's salary for me at the time.

My mind was racing as I drove home. I had believed that success would come to anyone who poured himself into his career. Curt helped me to realize that the key was personal growth. It occurred to me that if you focus on goals, you may hit goals—but that doesn't guarantee growth. If you focus on growth, you will grow and always hit goals.

As I drove, a quote from James Allen's *As a Man Thinketh* came to mind. I had first read that book in seventh grade and had subsequently read it nearly a dozen times. Allen wrote, "People are anxious to improve their circumstances but are unwilling to improve themselves; they therefore remain bound." I couldn't afford what Curt was offering. Yet in my heart I knew that he had uncovered the key to the ability to meet my next leadership challenge and go to the higher levels in my career. I could see the gap between where I was and where I wanted to be—where I needed to be! It was a growth gap, and I needed to figure out how to bridge it.

Growth Gap Traps

If you have dreams, goals, or aspirations, you need to grow to achieve them. But if you're like I was—and if you're like most people—you have one or more mistaken beliefs that create a gap that keeps you from growing and reaching your potential. Take a look at the following eight misconceptions about growth that may be holding you back from being as intentional as you need to be.

1. The Assumption Gap—"I Assume That I Will Automatically Grow"

When we are children, our bodies grow automatically. A year goes by, and we become taller, stronger, more capable of doing new things and facing new challenges. I think many people carry into adulthood a subconscious belief that mental, spiritual, and emotional growth follows a similar pattern. Time goes by, and we simply get better. We're like Charlie Brown in Charles Schulz's *Peanuts* comic strip, who once said, "I think I've discovered the secret of life—you just hang around until you get used to it." The problem is that we don't improve by simply living. We have to be intentional about it.

Musician Bruce Springsteen commented, "A time comes when you need to stop waiting for the man you want to become and start being the man you want to be." No one improves by accident. Personal growth doesn't just happen on its own. And once you're done with your formal education, you must take complete ownership of the growth process, because

> "A time comes when you need to stop waiting for the man you want to become and start being the man you want to be."
>
> —Bruce Springsteen

nobody else will do it for you. As Michel de Montaigne observed, "No wind favors him who has no destined port." If you want your life to improve, you must improve yourself. You must make that a tangible target.

2. The Knowledge Gap—"I Don't Know How to Grow"

After my meeting with Curt Kampmeier, I talked to everybody I knew and asked the same question Curt had asked me: "Do you have a growth plan?" I was hoping that somebody had figured this out and I could simply learn from him. Not one person said yes. Nobody in my world had a plan for growing and improving. I didn't know how to grow, and neither did they.

Designer, artist, and consultant Loretta Staples says, "If you are clear with what you want, the world responds with clarity." I knew what I wanted. I wanted to grow into the new job I was taking. I wanted to become someone capable of accomplishing the big goals I had set for myself. I just needed a way to do that.

Many people learn only from the school of hard knocks. Difficult experiences teach them lessons "the hard way," and they change—sometimes for the better, sometimes for the worse. The lessons are random and difficult. It's much better to *plan* your growth intentionally. You decide where you need or want to grow, you choose what you will learn, and you follow through with discipline going at the pace you set.

After I met with Curt and came to realize that I didn't know anyone else who could help me, my wife, Margaret, and I talked about ways we could scrimp, save, and go without to put aside $799. (You have to remember that this was before credit cards!) I skipped lunches. We canceled the vacation we had planned to take. We made do. It took us six months, but finally we did it. You can't imagine my excitement as I opened up the growth kit and started to flip through the five areas it covered: attitude, goals, discipline, measurement, and consistency.

I look back now and I can see how basic those things were that the kit taught me. But that's what I needed. Learning those lessons opened the door of personal growth a crack for me. And through that crack I began to see growth opportunities everywhere. My world began to open up. I accomplished more. I learned more. I was able to lead and help others more. Other opportunities began to present themselves. My world expanded. Outside of my faith, the decision to grow has impacted my life more than any other.

> Outside of my faith, the decision to grow has impacted my life more than any other.

3. The Timing Gap—"It's Not the Right Time to Begin"

When I was a kid, one of my father's favorite riddles to us went like this: Five frogs are sitting on a log. Four decide to jump off. How many are left?

The first time he asked me, I answered, "One."

"No," he responded. "Five. Why? Because there's a difference between deciding and doing!"

That was a point that Dad often drove home with us. American politician Frank Clark said, "What great accomplishments we'd have in the world if everybody had done what they intended to do." Most people don't act as quickly as they should on things. They find themselves subject to the Law of Diminishing Intent, which says, "The longer you wait to do something you should do now, the greater the odds that you will never actually do it."

> The Law of Diminishing Intent says, "The longer you wait to do something you should do now, the greater the odds that you will never actually do it."

Back when I was deciding whether to try to buy that first personal-growth plan, in a way I was lucky because I knew I was headed to a job where I would be in way over my head. I would be challenged beyond anything I'd ever done before. I would be under a microscope, with high expectations (some for me to succeed, some for me to fail) from everyone who knew me. And I knew that if I didn't get better as a leader, I would fail. That prompted me to act as quickly as I could.

You may be under similar personal or professional pressure right now. If you are, you're probably anxious to start growing and developing. But what if you're not? Whether you feel prompted to or not, now is the time to start growing. Author and professor Leo Buscaglia asserted, "Life lived for tomorrow will always be a day away from being realized." The reality is that you will never get much done unless you go ahead and do it before you are ready. If you're not already intentionally growing, you need to get started today. If you don't, you may reach some goals, which you can celebrate, but you will eventually plateau. Once you start growing intentionally, you can keep growing and keep asking "What's next?"

4. The Mistake Gap—"I'm Afraid of Making Mistakes"

Growing can be a messy business. It means admitting you don't have the answers. It requires making mistakes. It can make you look foolish. Most people don't enjoy that. But that is the price of admission if you want to improve.

Years ago I read a quote by Robert H. Schuller, who said, "What would you attempt to do if you knew you wouldn't fail?" Those words encouraged me to try things that I believed were beyond my capabilities. They also inspired me to write the book *Failing Forward*. When I received the first copy of that book from the publisher, I immediately wrote a thank-you in it to Dr. Schuller and signed it to him. And I made a trip to Garden Grove so I could present it to him and thank him for the positive influence he had on my life. A photograph that was taken of us on that day sits on the desk in my office as a reminder of his investment in me.

If you want to grow, you need to get over any fear you may have of making mistakes. As author and professor Warren Bennis asserts, "A mistake is simply another way of doing things." To become intentional about growing, expect to make mistakes every day, and welcome them as a sign that you are moving in the right direction.

> "A mistake is simply another way of doing things."
> —*Warren Bennis*

5. The Perfection Gap—"I Have to Find the Best Way Before I Start"

Similar to the Mistake Gap is the Perfection Gap, the desire to find the "best" way to get started in a growth plan. When Curt presented me with the idea of a growth plan, I went looking for the best way. But what I discovered is that I had it backward. I had to get started if I wanted to find the best way. It's similar to driving on an unfamiliar road at night. Ideally, you'd like to be able to see your whole route before you begin. But you see it progressively. As you move forward, a little more of the road is revealed to you. If you want to see more of the way, then get moving.

6. The Inspiration Gap—"I Don't Feel Like Doing It"

Many years ago, I was stuck in a doctor's waiting room for a really long time—so long, in fact, that I had completed all the work I'd brought with me for the wait and was looking for something productive to do. I flipped through a medical journal and found the following text, which has become one of my favorite examples of the inertia of motivation (and by the way, this was before Nike coined the phrase):

Just Do It
We hear it almost every day; sigh, sigh, sigh.
I just can't get myself motivated to... (lose weight, test my blood sugar, etc.) And we hear an equal number of sighs from diabetes educa-

tors who can't get their patients motivated to do the right things for their diabetes and health.

We have news for you. Motivation is not going to strike you like lightning. And motivation is not something that someone else—nurse, doctor, family member—can bestow or force on you. The whole idea of motivation is a trap. Forget motivation. Just *do it*.

Exercise, lose weight, test your blood sugar, or whatever. Do it without motivation and then guess what. After you start doing the thing, that's when the motivation comes and makes it easy for you to keep on doing it.

Motivation is like love and happiness. It's a by-product. When you're actively engaged in doing something, it sneaks up and zaps you when you least expect it.

As Harvard psychologist Jerome Bruner says, "You're more likely to act yourself into feeling than feel yourself into action." So act! Whatever it is you know you should do, do it.

When Curt suggested I needed to be intentional about growing, I had thousands of reasons *not* to do it. I didn't have the time, the money, the experience, and so on. I had only one reason *to* do it. I believed I *should* do it because I hoped it would make a difference. That certainly didn't feel inspirational. But I started. To my astonishment, after a year of dedicated growth, I started to pass some of my heroes. My reason for putting in the work changed from getting *started* to *staying* with it, because it *did* make a difference. After that, I didn't want to miss a single day!

You may not feel inspired to aggressively pursue a growth plan if you haven't started yet. If that's the case, please trust me when I say that the reasons to keep growing far outweigh the reasons to start growing. And you discover the reasons to stay with growth only if you stick with it long enough to start reaping the benefits. So make a commitment to yourself to start *and* stick with it for at least twelve months. If you do, you will fall in love with the process, and you will be able to look back at the end of that year and see how far you've come.

7. The Comparison Gap—"Others Are Better Than I Am"

Fairly early in my career, I attended an idea exchange with three other leaders in Orlando, Florida. I went because at the time I realized that I needed to be exposed to bigger and better leaders outside of my own small circle. At first when I arrived, I was intimidated. As we talked and shared ideas, it became clear very quickly that I was not in their league. Their organizations were six times the size of mine, and they had many more and much better ideas than I did. I felt like I was in over my head and trying to swim. Despite that, I was encouraged. Why? Because I discovered that great men were willing to share their ideas. And I was learning so much. You can learn only if others are ahead of you.

The first ten years that I was intentionally pursuing personal growth, I was always behind trying to catch up. I had to get over the comparison gap. I had to learn to become comfortable with being out of my comfort zone. It was a difficult transition, but it was well worth it.

8. The Expectation Gap—"I Thought It Would Be Easier Than This"

I don't know any successful person who thinks growth comes quickly and climbing to the top is easy. It just doesn't happen. People create their own luck. How? Here's the formula:

Preparation (growth) + **Attitude** + **Opportunity** + **Action** (doing something about it) = **Luck**

It all starts with preparation. Unfortunately, that takes time. But here's the best news. As Jim Rohn said, "You cannot change your destination over-

> "You cannot change your destination overnight, but you can change your direction overnight."
> —Jim Rohn

night, but you can change your direction overnight." If you want to reach your goals and fulfill your potential, become intentional about personal growth. It will change your life.

Making the Transition to Intentional Growth

The sooner you make the transition to becoming intentional about your personal growth, the better it will be for you, because growth compounds and accelerates if you *remain* intentional about it. Here's how to make the change:

1. Ask the Big Question Now

The first year that I engaged in intentional personal growth, I discovered that it was going to be a lifetime process. During that year, the question in my mind changed from "How long will this take?" to "How far can I go?" That is the question you should be asking yourself right now—not that you will be able to answer it. I started this growth journey forty years ago, and I still haven't answered it. But it will help you set the *direction*, if not the distance.

Where do you want to go in life?

What direction do you want to go?

What's the farthest you can imagine going?

Answering those questions will get you started on the personal-growth journey. The best you can hope to do in life is to make the most out of whatever you've been given. You do that by investing in yourself, making yourself the best you can be. The more you've got to work with, the greater your potential—and the farther you should try to go. As my dad used to say to me repeatedly when I was a kid, "To whomever much is given—much shall be required." Give growing your best so you can become your best.

2. Do It Now

In 1974 I attended a seminar at the University of Dayton, where W. Clement Stone spoke on the subject of having a sense of urgency. Stone was a business tycoon who had made his fortune in insurance. His session was titled "Do It Now," and one of the things he told us was this: "Before you get out of bed every morning, say 'do it now' fifty times. At the end of the day before you go to sleep, the last thing you should do is say 'do it now' fifty times."

I'm guessing there were about eight thousand people in the audience that day, but it felt like he was talking to me personally. I went home, and for the next six months I actually followed his advice. The first thing every morning and the last thing before I went to sleep, I repeated the words "do it now." It gave me a tremendous sense of urgency.

The greatest danger you face in this moment is the idea that you will make intentional growth a priority *later*. Don't fall into that trap! Recently I read an article by Jennifer Reed in *SUCCESS*. She wrote,

> Can there be a more insidious word? Later, as in "I'll do it later." Or, "Later, I'll have time to write that book that's been on my mind for the past five years." Or, "I know I need to straighten out my finances... I'll do it later."
>
> "Later" is one of those dream-killers, one of the countless obstacles we put up to derail our chances of success. The diet that starts "tomorrow," the job hunt that happens "eventually," the pursuit of the life dream that begins "someday" combine with other self-imposed roadblocks and lock us on autopilot.
>
> Why do we do this to ourselves, anyway? Why don't we take action now? Let's face it: The familiar is easy; the uncharted path is lined with uncertainties.[1]

By starting to read this book, you've already begun the process. Don't stop there! Keep taking more steps. Pick a resource that will help you grow and begin learning from it *today*.

3. Face the Fear Factor

I recently read an article on the fears that keep people from being successful. The following five factors came into play:

Fear of Failure
Fear of Trading Security for the Unknown
Fear of Being Overextended Financially
Fear of What Others Will Say or Think
Fear that Success Will Alienate Peers

Which of those fears most impacts you? For me it was the last one: alienating my peers. By nature I'm a people pleaser, and I wanted everyone to like me. But it really doesn't matter which fear affects you the most. We all have fears. But here's the good news. We also all have faith. The question you have to ask yourself is, "Which emotion will I allow to be stronger?" Your answer is important, because the stronger emotion wins. I want to encourage you to feed your faith and starve your fear.

4. Change from Accidental to Intentional Growth

People tend to get into ruts in life. They get in an easy groove, and they don't try to break out if it—even when it's taking them in the wrong direction. After a while, they just get by. If they learn something, it's because of a happy accident. Don't let that happen to you! If that is the attitude you've developed, then you would do well to remember that the only difference between a rut and a grave is the length!

How do you know if you've slipped into a rut? Take a look at the differences between accidental growth and intentional growth:

ACCIDENTAL GROWTH	INTENTIONAL GROWTH
Plans to Start Tomorrow	Insists on Starting Today
Waits for Growth to Come	Takes Complete Responsibility to Grow
Learns Only from Mistakes	Often Learns Before Mistakes
Depends on Good Luck	Relies on Hard Work
Quits Early and Often	Perseveres Long and Hard
Falls into Bad Habits	Fights for Good Habits
Talks Big	Follows Through
Plays It Safe	Takes Risks
Thinks Like a Victim	Thinks Like a Learner
Relies on Talent	Relies on Character
Stops Learning after Graduation	Never Stops Growing

Eleanor Roosevelt said, "One's philosophy is not best expressed in words; it is expressed in the choices one makes. In the long run, we shape our lives and we shape ourselves. The process never ends until we die. And the choices we make are ultimately our own responsibility."

"One's philosophy is not best expressed in words; it is expressed in the choices one makes. In the long run, we shape our lives and we shape ourselves."

—*Eleanor Roosevelt*

If you want to reach your potential and become the person you were created to be, you must do much more than just experience life and hope that you learn what you need along the way. You must go out of your way to seize growth opportunities as if your future depended on it. Why? Because it does. Growth doesn't just happen—not for me, not for you, not for anybody. You have to go after it!

Applying
the Law of Intentionality
to Your Life

1. Which of the gaps discussed in the chapter have caused you to neglect growing the way you perhaps could have?

❑ The Assumption Gap—I assume that I will automatically grow.

❑ The Knowledge Gap—I don't know how to grow.

❑ The Timing Gap—It's not the right time to begin.

❑ The Mistake Gap—I'm afraid of making mistakes.

❑ The Perfection Gap—I have to find the best way before I start.

❑ The Inspiration Gap—I don't feel like doing it.

❑ The Comparison Gap—Others are better than I am.

❑ The Expectation Gap—I thought it would be easier than this.

Now that you have gained insight about the gaps, what strategies can you create and implement to help you bridge the gaps? Write a specific plan for each gap that applied to you and take the first step of that plan *today.*

2. Most people underestimate the unimportance of nearly everything in their lives. They get distracted. As a result, they put growth on the back burner, and if they do grow, it happens accidentally instead of intentionally. Take a look at your calendar for the next twelve months. How much time have you specifically scheduled for personal growth? If you're like most people, your answer will be none. Or you may have planned to attend one event in the coming year. That's not going to cut it.

Rework your calendar so you have an appointment with yourself for personal growth every day, five days a week, fifty weeks a year. You might be thinking, *What? I don't have time for that!* That's probably true. Do it anyway. If you want to succeed, you need to do whatever it takes. Get up an hour early. Stay up an hour later. Give up your lunch hour. Put in extra time on the weekends. If you don't, you'll have to prepare to give up your dreams and any hope of reaching your potential.

3. Start now. No matter what time of day you're reading these words, make a commitment to start growing today. Give that first hour before you go to sleep tonight. Put in the time today and for the next five days. You probably won't feel like doing it. Do it anyway.

2

The Law of Awareness

You Must Know Yourself to Grow Yourself

"No one can produce great things who is not thoroughly sincere in dealing with himself."
—JAMES RUSSELL LOWELL

In 2004, Adam Sandler and Drew Barrymore starred in a comedy called *50 First Dates*. It is the story of a man who falls in love with a young woman, only to discover that she cannot remember him the next day. In fact, she can't remember anything that has happened to her since a car crash she was in a year before. She is destined to live every day as if it were the day before her accident. It was a cute movie, even if the premise seems a bit silly. But what if something like that were true and had actually happened?

No Recall

There is a famous neuropsychology case of someone with a similar condition that was first docu-
mented in 1957 and has been studied by thousands of
doctors and researchers. The patient is called Henry
M. He was born in Hartford, Connecticut, in 1926,
and he suffered from a case of epilepsy that was so
severe and debilitating that he couldn't function. At
age twenty-seven, he underwent an experimental surgery in which parts of his brain were removed to try
to treat his epilepsy. The good news was that after the
surgery, he no longer suffered constant debilitating
seizures. In addition, he suffered no negative impact
on his intelligence, personality, or ability to interact
with others socially. However, there was one horrible
side effect. He seemed to have no short-term memory.

Henry M. couldn't remember anything that happened after the surgery. He didn't recognize his doctors. He couldn't find his way to the bathroom. When
he returned home, he would do the same jigsaw puzzles every day and read the same magazines without
having any memory of having done so. When his
family moved to a new house, he could never remember having moved, nor could he find the way to his
new home, though he remembered his old one viv-

idly. When interviewed thirty minutes after lunch, he could not recall a single item he had eaten. In fact, he could not remember having eaten at all.[1] He was stuck in time, unable to learn, grow, and change. What a tragedy.

Do You Have a Sense of Direction?

Any person who wants to grow but doesn't know himself is in many ways like Henry M. To grow, you must know yourself: your strengths and weaknesses, your interests and opportunities. You must be able to gauge not only where you've been, but also where you are now. Otherwise you cannot set a course for where you want to go. And of course, every time you want to learn something, you must be able to take the new thing you've learned today and build upon what you learned yesterday to keep growing. That's the only way to gain traction and keep improving yourself.

To reach your potential, you must know where you want to go and where you currently are. Without both of those pieces of information, you're liable to get lost. Knowing yourself is like reading "You Are Here" on a map when you want to find your way to a destination.

I've observed that there are really only three kinds of people when it comes to having direction in life:

1. People Who Don't Know What They Would Like to Do

These people are often *confused*. They lack a strong sense of purpose. They don't possess a sense of direction for their lives. If they are growing, they are unfocused about it. They dabble. They drift. They can't reach their potential because they have no idea what to shoot for.

2. People Who Know What They Would Like to Do But Don't Do It

These people are usually *frustrated*. Every day they experience the gap between where they are and where they want to be. Sometimes they aren't doing what they want because they worry that it will cause them to neglect other responsibilities, such as providing for their families. Sometimes they aren't willing to pay the price to learn, grow, and move closer to where they want to be. Other times fear prevents them from changing course to pursue their passion. No matter what the reason, they, too, miss their potential.

3. People Who Know What They Would Like to Do and Do It

The third kind of people know themselves, possess a strong sense of passion, are focused in purpose, grow in areas that help them move closer to their purpose, and do what they were created to do. The word that best describes them is *fulfilled*.

Few situations are as extreme as Henry M.'s, yet most people seem to fall into the first category. They don't know what they want to do. I believe the main reason is that they don't know themselves as well as they should, and thus remain unfocused in their growth.

Knowing yourself isn't necessarily an easy thing for everyone to do. In a commencement address at Princeton, future American president Woodrow Wilson proclaimed,

> We live in an age disturbed, confused, bewildered, afraid of its own forces, in search not merely of its road but even of its direction. There are many voices of counsel, but few voices of vision; there is much excitement and feverish activity, but little concert of thoughtful purpose. We are distressed by our ungoverned, undirected energies and do many things, but nothing long. It is our duty to find ourselves.

Wilson made that statement in 1907! Imagine what he might have said if he were alive today.

> You have to know who you are to grow to your potential. But you have to grow in order to know who you are.

What makes finding themselves and growing to their potential difficult for some people is that it can be a bit of a catch-22. You have to know who you are to grow to your potential. But you have to grow in order to know who you are. So what's the solution? Explore yourself as you explore growth.

The way to start is to pay attention to your passions. For me, that started when I focused my growth in areas that I knew would help me as a minister, which was my passion. The four areas can be represented by the word REAL: relationships, equipping, attitude, and leadership. My passion led to my growth. But then my growth led to my passion, as I discovered my love and ability for leadership. That has continued to be a major focus of my personal growth for nearly forty years. Other areas that passion and purpose revealed include faith, family, communication, and creativity. All of these continue to be important parts of my life where I love to learn and to grow.

How to Find Your Passion and Purpose

Psychotherapist Nathaniel Branden asserts, "The first step toward change is awareness. The second

step is acceptance." If you
want to change and grow,
then you must know your-
self and accept who you are
before you can start building.

> "The first step toward change is awareness. The second step is acceptance."
> —*Nathaniel Branden*

Here are ten questions to help
you start working through that process.

1. Do You Like What You're Doing Now?

I am amazed by how many people I meet every
day who don't like doing what they do for a living.
Why do they do it? I understand the necessity of having to make a living. We've all done jobs we didn't
love. I worked in a meat-packing plant when I was in
college. I didn't like that job. But I didn't stay there
my whole life, doing something I found unfulfilling.
If I'd loved it and it had fit my passion and purpose,
I would have stayed there and tried to build a career.
But it wasn't what I wanted to do.

Philosopher Abraham Kaplan noted, "If, as Socrates
said, the unexamined life is not worth living, so the
unlived life is worth examining." If you're not enjoying
what you do for a living, you need to take some time to
examine why.

Is it a risk making a change from what you're currently doing to what you *want* to do? Of course. You
might fail. You might find out that you don't like it as

much as you expected. You might not make as much money. But isn't there also great risk in staying where you are? You might fail. You might get fired. You might take a pay cut. Or worst of all, you might come to the end of your life feeling regret for never having reached your potential or doing what you love. Which risk would you rather live with?

2. What Would You Like to Do?

There is definitely a direct connection between finding your passion and reaching your potential. TV journalist Maria Bartiromo says, "Every successful person I've met has a strong sense of his or her unique abilities and aspirations. They're leaders in their own lives, and they dare to pursue their dreams on their own terms."

> There is definitely a direct connection between finding your passion and reaching your potential.

Have you found and harnessed your passion? Do you know what you would like to do? When you do, it makes all the difference. Why? When you tap into your passion, it gives you the E&E factor: *energy* and *excellence*.

- You will never fulfill your destiny doing work you despise.

- Passion gives you an advantage over others, because one person with passion is greater than ninety-nine who have only an interest!
- Passion gives you energy.

As a kid, all I ever wanted to do was play. I didn't like work. But I learned the power of tapping into my passion when I transitioned from high school to college. In high school, I was simply marking time. But when I got to college, I was working in areas connected to my purpose. I was pursuing my passion. That got me excited!

I'm still excited about what I do. Now that I'm in my midsixties, people ask me when I will retire. To be honest, that's not on my radar. Why would anyone want to quit doing what he loves? Nothing's work unless you'd rather be doing something else. Want to know when I'll retire? When I die! That's when I'll stop speaking and writing books.

How do you *know* what you want to do? How do you tap into your passion? Listen to your heart. Pay attention to what you love doing. Pulitzer Prize–winning journalist and author Thomas L. Friedman advises,

So whatever you plan to do, whether you plan to travel the world next year, go to graduate school, join the workforce, or take some time off to think, don't just listen to your head. Listen to your heart. It's the best career counselor there is. Do what you really love to do and if you don't know quite what that is yet, well, keep searching, because if you find it, you'll bring that something extra to your work that will help ensure you will not be automated or outsourced. It will help make you an untouchable radiologist, an untouchable engineer, or an untouchable teacher.

If you never figure out what you want to do, you will probably be frustrated all of your life. Author Stephen Covey observed, "How different our lives are when we really know what is deeply important to us, and keeping that picture in mind, we manage ourselves each day to be and to know what matters most." Knowing yourself and what you want to do is one of the most important things you'll ever do in this life.

3. Can You Do What You Would Like to Do?

When I was a minister, I once had a young man named Bobby working for me. He was my worship leader. If you're unfamiliar with that role, it's the person who prepares the music for a Sunday service, leads the other singers and musicians, and actually leads the congregation in singing.

I could see that Bobby was an unhappy person, and I suspected that he would rather be doing something different. So one day I sat him down for a heart-to-heart talk. He confessed that he was really unhappy. I asked him, "Bobby, what would you like to do?"

He hesitated a moment and then confided, "I'd really like to be the announcer for the Chicago Cubs baseball team."

All I could think was *You're going to be unhappy for a very long time.* He didn't have the skills to do that job. Even if he did, the job wasn't available! I told him he needed to find something more realistic that aligned with his gifting and opportunities.

There's a big difference between having a dream that propels you to achieve and pulling an idea out of thin air that has no connection with who you are and what you can do. I feel so strongly about helping people with this problem that I wrote a book about it called *Put Your Dream to the Test.* You must have some kind of criteria for knowing if the desire you have matches the abilities you possess.

> You must have some kind of criteria for knowing if the desire you have matches the abilities you possess.

Warren Bennis has also

developed something to help people with this issue. He offers three questions you can ask yourself to identify if what you want to do is possible. Ask yourself:

- *Do you know the difference between what you want and what you're good at?* These two things don't always match up. I believe that was the case for Bobby. What he wanted and what he could do were two very different things. To be successful, you need to be doing what you're good at.

- *Do you know what drives you and what gives you satisfaction?* Sometimes people get it in their heads to do something for the wrong reasons. Maybe the job they want doesn't look like hard work, when in fact it is. Or they want the rewards that come with the job, not the work itself. When what motivates you lines up with what satisfies you, it is a powerful combination.

- *Do you know what your values and priorities are, and what your organization's values and priorities are?* The more you can align these two, the greater your chance of success. If you and your employer are working at cross-purposes, success will be difficult to achieve.

Measuring the differences between what you want and what you're able to do, what drives you and what satisfies you, and your values and those of the organization reveals many of the obstacles between you and what you want to do. At that point the question you need to ask yourself is whether you are able to overcome those differences.

One of the main keys to being successful and fulfilling your purpose is to understand your unique talents and to find the right arena in which to use them. Some people have an inherent ability to know who they are and who they're not. Others have to work hard to make those discoveries. Poet and critic Samuel Johnson observed, "Almost every man wastes part of his life in attempts to display qualities which he does not possess." Your goal should be to waste as little of your life as possible. As former MLB catcher Jim Sundberg says, "Discover your uniqueness; then discipline yourself to develop it."

> "Almost every man wastes part of his life in attempts to display qualities which he does not possess."
>
> —Samuel Johnson

4. Do You Know Why You Want to Do What You Would Like to Do?

I believe it's very important not only to know what you want to do, but also why you want to do it. I say that because motives matter. When you do things for the right reason, it gives you inner strength when things go wrong. Right motives help you to build positive relationships because they prevent hidden agendas and incline you to put people ahead of your agenda. Doing something for the right reasons also keeps life less cluttered and your path clearer. Not only is your vision clearer, but you also sleep well at night knowing you're on the right track.

The work that I do is a calling on my life. When I lead or communicate, I think, *I was born for this*. It relies on my strengths. It gives me energy. It makes a difference in the lives of others. It fulfills me and gives me a touch of the eternal.

I believe you can have the same kind of satisfaction and can experience success if you do the things you were meant to do, and do them for the right reasons. Take time to reflect. Explore your intentions and attitudes. As psychiatrist Carl Jung advised, "Your vision will become clear only when you look into your heart. Who looks outside, dreams. Who looks inside, awakens."

> "Your vision will become clear only when you look into your heart. Who looks outside, dreams. Who looks inside, awakens."
>
> —Carl Jung

The first four questions you should ask yourself relate to *what* you want to do. As I said at the beginning of the chapter, you must know yourself to grow yourself. That's the Law of Awareness. But I want to help you to do more than just know what to do. I want you to have a sense of *how* to start moving in that direction. That will help you to target and eventually fine-tune your growth. With that in mind, the remaining questions will help you to create a game plan.

5. Do You Know What to Do So You Can Do What You Want to Do?

To move from what you're doing now to what you want to do is a process. Do you know what it will take? I believe it begins with...

AWARENESS

Darren Hardy, the publisher of *SUCCESS* magazine, says, "Picture where you are in [any] area, right now. Now picture where you want to be: richer, thinner, happier, you name it. The first step toward change is awareness. If you want to get from where you are to where you want to be, you have to start by becoming aware of the choices that lead you away from your desired destination. Become very conscious of every choice you make today so you can begin to make smarter choices moving forward."

You cannot change direction if you aren't aware that you're not headed where you want to go. That probably sounds obvious. But have you taken the time to look at where your current choices and activities are taking you? Spend some time really thinking about where you're presently headed. If it's not where you want to go, then write out what steps you need to take to go where you desire to go, to do what you want to do. Make them as tangible as possible. Will they definitely be the *right* steps? Maybe, maybe not. But you won't know for sure until you start moving forward. And that takes us to the next phase:

ACTION

You cannot win if you do not begin! The people who get ahead in the world are the ones who look for the circumstances they want, and if they can't find them, they make them. That means taking initiative. It means doing something specific every day that will take you another step closer to your goal. It means continuing to do it every day. Nearly all successes are the fruit of initiative.

> You cannot win if you do not begin! The people who get ahead in the world are the ones who look for the circumstances they want, and if they can't find them, they make them.

ACCOUNTABILITY

Few things prompt a person to follow through like accountability. One of the ways you can do that is to make your goals public. When you tell others about what you intend to do, it puts pressure on you to keep working at it. You can request that specific individuals ask you about your progress. It's similar to having a deadline to keep you moving. You can even write things down as a form of accountability. That's what Darren Hardy suggests. He says that you should track every action that pertains to an area where you want to see improvement, whether it relates to finances, health, career, or relationships. "Simply carry around a small notebook, something you'll keep in your pocket or purse at all times, and a writing instrument," says Hardy. "You're going to write it all down. Every day. Without fail. No excuses, no exceptions. As if Big Brother's watching you. Doesn't sound like much fun, I know—writing things down on a little piece of paper. But tracking *my* progress and missteps is one of the reasons I've accumulated the success I have. The process forces you to be conscious of your decisions."

ATTRACTION

If you become aware of the steps you must take to do what you want to do, take action, and become accountable for following through, you will begin to produce the behavior you desire and you will start getting closer to doing what you want to do. And that will start to result in a positive side effect: You start attracting like-minded people. The Law of Magnetism in *The 21 Irrefutable Laws of Leadership* says, "Who you are is who you attract." That is true in leadership, but it is also true in every other aspect of life. As my mother used to say, "Birds of a feather flock together."

If you want to be around growing people, become a growing person. If you're committed, you attract others who are committed. If you're growing, you attract others who are growing. This puts you in a position to begin building a community of like-minded people who can help one another succeed.

6. Do You Know People Who Do What You'd Like to Do?

My greatest growth has always come as a result of finding people ahead of me who were able to show me the way forward. Some of them have helped me through personal contact, but most have helped through the books they've written. When I've had questions, I've found answers in their wisdom. When I wanted to learn how to lead better, I looked to Melvin Maxwell, Bill Hybels, John Wooden, Oswald Sanders, Jesus Christ, and hundreds of others to show me the way. If I've learned how to communicate more effectively, it is because I've learned from Andy Stanley, Johnny Carson, Howard Hendricks, Ronald Reagan, Billy Graham, and hundreds of others. If I create and write in a way that helps people, it is because Les Stobbe, Max Lucado, Charlie Wetzel, Les Parrott, Bob Buford, and others have spent time with me.

If you have discovered what you want to do, start finding people who do what you want to do with excellence. Then do what you must to learn from them.

Get committed. Pay people for their time if necessary.

Be consistent. Meet purposefully every month with someone who can teach you.

Be creative. Start with their books if you can't meet them in person.

Be purposeful. Spend two hours in preparation for every hour of interaction.

Be reflective. Spend two hours in reflection for every hour of interaction.

Be grateful. These people are gifts to your personal growth; be sure to let them know.

Always remember that you cannot get where you want to go on your own. You will need the help of others to guide you on your way.

7. Should You Do What You'd Like to Do with Them?

If you are someone who is dedicated to personal growth, you will always be learning from many people in many places. Occasionally you will have an opportunity to be mentored on an ongoing basis by an individual. Being mentored by someone who is successful in your area of interest has great value, and I will discuss it more thoroughly in the Law of Modeling chapter. However, I pause now to give you advice as you approach a mentor. If you find a potential mentor, know that the following are your responsibility:

- Possess a teachable spirit.
- Always be prepared for the time you get with your mentor.
- Set the agenda by asking great questions.
- Demonstrate how you've learned from your time together.
- Be accountable for what you've learned.

As someone who has mentored a lot of people, I can tell you what I think the responsibilities of a mentor are. My responsibility to the people I mentor is to add value. My goal is always to help them to become more than they are, not to try to make them something they're not. These are the areas I focus on:

- Strengths
- Temperament
- Track record
- Passion
- Choices

- Advice
- Support, Resources/People
- Game plan
- Feedback
- Encouragement

For each of these areas, think about what specific contribution you can offer to the person you are mentoring.

One of the people I have enjoyed investing in is Courtney McBath of Norfolk, Virginia. The second time I met with him, he said the following:

Here's what I asked.
Here's what you shared.
Here's what I did.
Now can I ask more questions?

With someone who follows though like that, my answer is always yes!

Every person who *can* help you is not necessarily the right person *to* help you. You must pick and choose. And so must they. Your goal should be to find a fit that is mutually beneficial for both mentor and mentee.

8. Will You Pay the Price to Do What You Want to Do?

Author and educator James Thom said, "Probably the most honest self-made man ever was the one we heard say: 'I got to the top the hard way—fighting my own laziness and ignorance every step of the way.'" That sure has a lot of truth in it, doesn't it? When it comes to barriers to success, we are usually our own worst enemies.

Several years ago, I came across a piece called "Dream Big." It's full of encouraging words but also captures what it takes to follow your dreams. It says,

> *If there were ever a time to dare,*
> *To make a difference,*
> *To embark on something worth doing,*
> *It is now.*
> *Not for any grand cause, necessarily—*
> *But for something that tugs at your heart,*
> *Something that's your aspiration,*
> *Something that's your dream.*
> *You owe it to yourself to make your days here count.*
> *Have fun.*

Dig deep.
Stretch.
Dream big.
Know, though, that things worth doing seldom
    come easy.
There will be good days.
And there will be bad days.
There will be times when you want to turn around,
Pack it up, and call it quits.
Those times tell you that you are pushing yourself,
That you are not afraid to learn by trying.[2]

Taking the steps necessary to live your dreams and do what you want to do will cost you. You will have to work hard. You will have to make sacrifices. You will have to keep learning and growing and changing. Are you willing to pay that price? I certainly hope you are. But know this: Most people aren't.

9. When Can You Start Doing What You'd Like to Do?

Ask people when they will do what they want to do, and most answer that they hope to do it "someday." Why not now? Because you're not ready? Perhaps you're not. But if you wait until you are, maybe you never will do it.

> Most of the accomplishments I've achieved in life I began to attempt before I was really ready.

Most of the accomplishments I've achieved in life I began to attempt before I was really ready. When I was teaching pastors leadership in 1984 and they asked for ongoing teaching, I wasn't ready to give it to them. But during a conference with thirty-four people in Jackson, Mississippi, I decided to pass around a legal pad and get the contact information for anyone who wanted to receive a monthly leadership tape. All thirty-four signed up. Was I ready to start a monthly leadership subscription series? No. Did I start it anyway? Yes. When I needed to raise money to relocate my church, did I know how to do it? No. Did I start to do it anyway? Yes. When I founded EQUIP to teach leadership to people in countries around the world, did I have a proven strategy to get it done? No. Did we get started anyway? Yes. Nobody ever got ready by waiting. You only get ready by starting.

10. What Will It Be Like When You Get to Do What You'd Like to Do?

Because I've had the privilege of doing what I've always wanted to do, I want to help you see ahead to what it's like. First, it will be *different* from what you imagined. I never thought that I would affect as many people as I do. I never knew life would be so beautiful. I never thought I would want to occasionally withdraw from people to think and write. But I also never anticipated the expectations others would put on me to produce.

When you do what you want to do, it will be *more difficult* than you ever imagined. I had no idea how much time it would take to be effective. I never expected to have such great demands put on my life or to have to keep paying the price to be successful. I also never dreamed that my energy level would go down as much as it has in recent years.

Finally, let me tell you this. When you do what you've always wanted to, it will be *better* than you ever imagined. When I started investing in my personal growth, I didn't anticipate a compounding return— for me personally, for the individuals I've mentored, and for my team. And I never dreamed it would be this much fun! Nothing else compares to doing what you were created to do.

A few years ago at Exchange, a leadership event I host for executives each year, we were privileged to have Coretta Scott King and Bernice King as two of our speakers. We all sat in the sanctuary at Ebenezer Baptist Church in Atlanta and listened to them tell

> There are two great days in a person's life: the day you were born and the day you discover why.

stories. What the Exchange attendees most wanted to know about was Martin Luther King Jr.'s "I Have a Dream" speech. Bernice told us that there were many speakers scheduled to address the crowd that day on the steps of the Lincoln Memorial. Many of them jockeyed for the best places in the speaking order, hoping to get TV time. Bernice's father gave up his time. He didn't care about his place on the docket. All he cared about was getting to communicate with the people. And when he did, it made history. Why? Because he was doing what he was made to do. The next year, the Civil Rights Act was passed in Washington, D.C. King had followed his passion, found his purpose, and as a result, made an impact on the world.

People say there are two great days in a person's life: the day you were born and the day you discover why. I want to encourage you to seek what you were put on this earth to do. Then pursue it with all your effort.

Applying
the Law of Awareness
to Your Life

The questions in this chapter are designed to prompt you to know yourself and get on course to do what you were made to do in life. Here is a streamlined version of the questions. Spend a significant amount of time answering them so you have a plan of action to follow when you're done.

1. What would you like to do?
2. What talents, skills, and opportunities do you possess that support your desire to do it?
3. What are your motives for wanting to do it?
4. What steps must you take (beginning today) to start doing what you want to do?:

   • Awareness
   • Action
   • Accountability

5. Whose advice can you get to help you along the way?

6. What price are you willing to pay? What will it cost you in time, resources, and sacrifices?

7. Where do you most need to grow? (You must focus on your strengths and overcome any weaknesses that would keep you from reaching your goal.)

3

The Law of the Mirror

You Must See Value in Yourself to Add Value to Yourself

"Personal development is the belief that you are worth the effort, time, and energy needed to develop yourself."
—DENIS WAITLEY

I often ask myself what keeps people from being successful. I believe all people have the seeds of success within them. All they need to do is cultivate those seeds, water them, feed them, and they will begin to grow. That is why I have spent my life trying to add value to people. I love to see people blossom!

So why do many people fail to grow and reach their potential? I've concluded that one of the main reasons is low self-esteem. Many people don't believe in themselves. They don't see the possibilities that God put in them. They possess a hundred acres of possibilities, yet never cultivate them because they are convinced that they won't be able to learn and grow and blossom into something wonderful.

Potential Squashed

That was the case of Johnnetta McSwain, whose story I recently learned about. For more than thirty years, she was someone who saw little value or potential in herself. But to be honest, there were many legitimate reasons for her poor perception of herself.

She was born to a single mother who didn't want her and told her so. She and her sister, Sonya, who was a year older, along with a cousin, spent the first five or six years of their lives being raised by their grandmother in Birmingham, Alabama. But the house was also shared by three uncles, who abused all three of the children psychologically, physically, and sexually. Johnnetta was scarred both physically and emotionally.

"By the time I was five years old," says Johnnetta, "I had already started to believe that I was not only inferior, but I was also a child abandoned by her own mamma. As a child, I had no place, no voice, and no worth at all."[1]

When Johnnetta and Sonya's mother learned about the abuse, she moved the three girls to a new home. But the abuse continued, this time from the men her mother brought home. Sonya ultimately responded by living on the streets and turning to crack cocaine. Johnnetta avoided drugs, but she spent much of her time on the streets and dropped out of high school in the eleventh grade. She had her first child out of wedlock at age nineteen, then a second child in her midtwenties. For the most part, she lived in government-supported housing and on government assistance, and relied on her boyfriends for additional support. To keep herself in designer clothes, she resorted to shoplifting.

Sonya's perspective poignantly sums up the state they were in: "Everybody in my family been in jail, on drugs, didn't finish high school, so what I got to live for? What I got to amount to? Nothing! What I got to accomplish? Nothing."[2]

A Look in the Mirror

Johnnetta's thirtieth birthday caused her to look in the mirror. She didn't like what she saw. She writes,

That day I woke up and realized I had absolutely nothing to celebrate—no money, no full-time job, no home, no husband, and no clue, not even the will to do better....At last, I knew it was time to make some changes.[3]

She wasn't happy with her life, and she realized that if she continued in the same direction she was going, her two sons would also be headed for trouble. As far as she knew, not a single male member of her family had ever finished high school. Many died young or ended up in jail. She didn't want that for her boys.

For Johnnetta, the process started with her working to get her GED. She took a twelve-week course to prepare and then took the test. She needed a score of 45 to pass. She received a 44.5. But she was determined to make something of herself, so she scheduled a retake at her first opportunity. When she passed, she was excited to be chosen to speak at the graduation ceremony. No one from her family bothered to attend.

Johnnetta knew that if she was going to change, she needed to leave Birmingham and get a fresh start. And she wanted to do something no one in her family had ever done—go to college. She decided to move to Atlanta, Georgia, and was motivated by a profound thought: "I get a chance to be anyone I want to be."[4]

> "I get a chance to be anyone I want to be."
> —Johnnetta McSwain

It took her almost three years to pull it off, but she made the move. Soon afterward, she enrolled in Kennesaw State University, deciding to take more than a full load every semester. She was thirty-three years old when she started school. She was street smart, but not very book smart—at least not at first. That intimidated her in the beginning. But for the first time in her life, she was determined to better herself. And soon she realized she could do it.

"I realized I didn't have to be smart," Johnnetta explains. "I just had to be determined, motivated, and focused. This came with a high price tag for me. I had to exchange my thinking. I had to think like a smart person."[5] Not only did she study hard and stay focused, but she also sought out the smartest person in each of her classes and asked to study with her. Soon she was studying and thinking like the best students in the school. She also maintained the vision she had for her future. At the beginning of every semester, she went to the bookstore on campus and tried on a cap and gown, looking at herself in the mirror and imagining what it would be like to graduate.

One day when a classmate was talking to her, she had a realization. The classmate was saying, "I don't love myself. I'm a nobody."

Johnnetta responded, "You sure can love you

if I love me." And that's when it hit her, maybe for the first time. "I realized I loved myself." She had changed. She was turning into the person she wanted to be, that she was created to be.

Johnnetta completed the work for a bachelor's degree in three years. Then she enrolled in graduate school, where she earned a master's degree in social work. Currently, she is working toward earning her doctorate.

"I went for something that society told me, 'You can't do,'" says Johnnetta. "Oh, yes I can!"[6]

The Power of Positive Self-Esteem

Johnnetta's story is a powerful example of what can happen in a person's life when she recognizes her value and begins to add value to herself. In Johnnetta's case, she was motivated by the desire to help her children, and she began to add value to herself *first*, and later saw the value in herself. It doesn't matter which occurs first. One feeds the other. What matters is that the cycle of value starts!

If you don't realize that you have genuine value and that you are worth investing in, then you will never put in the time and effort needed to grow to your potential. If you're not sure you agree with that, then consider the following.

Self-Esteem Is the Single Most Significant Key to a Person's Behavior

Often have I heard my friend Zig Ziglar say, "It's impossible to consistently behave in a manner inconsistent with how we see ourselves. We can do very few things in a positive way if we feel negative about ourselves." Zig has a very practical, commonsense wisdom that he has shared with people for years. But experts in the field agree with his assessment. Nathaniel Branden, a psychiatrist and expert on the subject of self-esteem, says, "No factor is more important in people's psychological development and motivation than the value judgments they make about themselves. Every aspect of their lives is impacted by the way they see themselves." If you believe you are worthless, then you won't add value to yourself.

> "No factor is more important in people's psychological development and motivation than the value judgments they make about themselves."
>
> —Nathaniel Branden

Low Self-Esteem Puts a Ceiling on Our Potential

I'm well known for teaching the Law of the Lid from *The 21 Irrefutable Laws of Leadership*. Imagine that you want to do something great in your life that impacts a lot of people. Perhaps you want to build a large organization. That desire, no matter how great, will be limited by your leadership. It is a lid on your potential. Well, your self-esteem has the same kind of impact. If your desire is a 10 but your self-esteem is a 5, you'll never perform at the level of a 10. You'll perform as a 5 or lower. People are never able to outperform their self-image. As Nathanial Branden says, "If you feel inadequate to face challenges, unworthy of love or respect, unentitled to happiness, and fear assertive thoughts, wants, or needs—if you lack basic self-trust, self-respect, and self-confidence—your self-esteem deficiency will limit you, no matter what other assets you possess."

> **People are never able to outperform their self-image.**

The Value We Place on Ourselves Is Usually the Value Others Place on Us

A man went to a fortune-teller to hear what she had to say about his future. She looked into a crystal ball and said, "You will be poor and unhappy until you are forty-five years old."

"Then what will happen?" asked the man hopefully.

"Then you'll get used to it."

I'm sorry to say, that's the way most people live their lives—according to what others believe about them. If the important people in their lives expect them to go nowhere, then that's what they expect for themselves. That's fine if you're surrounded by people who believe in you. But what if you're not?

You shouldn't become too concerned about what others might think of you. You should be more concerned about what you think of yourself. That's what Johnnetta McSwain did. As she prepared for her move to Atlanta, her friends and family told her it would never happen. When she did move, they told her she would fail and return to Birmingham. Nobody really believed in her. She didn't care. She had her own solution. She says, "You don't have to accept what people say you have to be."[7] Isn't that wonderful?

If you put a small value on yourself, rest assured the world will not raise the price. If you want to become the person you have the potential to be, you must believe you can!

Steps to Build Your Self-Image

I must admit that self-image has never been a problem for me. I grew up in a very positive environment, and I've always believed I could succeed. But I've worked with a lot of people who didn't. And I've been able to help some of them turn the corner and believe in themselves the way I believe in them. And I hope to

> If you put a small value on yourself, rest assured the world will not raise the price.

be able to help you too, if that's your situation. To get you started, please take to heart the following ten suggestions.

1. Guard Your Self-Talk

Whether you know it or not, you have a running conversation with yourself all the time. What is the nature of yours? Do you encourage yourself? Or do you criticize yourself? If you are positive, then you help to create a positive self-image. If you're negative, you undermine your self-worth. Where does negative, critical self-talk come from? Usually from our upbringing. In their book *The Answer*, businessmen-authors John Assaraf and Murray Smith talk about the negative messages children receive growing up. They write,

> By the time you're seventeen years old, you've heard "No, you can't," an average of 150,000 times. You've heard "Yes, you can," about 5,000 times. That's thirty nos for every yes. That makes for a powerful belief of "I can't."[8]

That's a lot to overcome. It's one of the reasons it took Johnnetta McSwain thirty years to start believing she could change. From an early age, she had been made to feel valueless.

If we want to change our lives, we have to change the way we think of ourselves. If we want to change the way we think of ourselves, we need to change the way we *talk* to ourselves. And the older we are, the more responsible we are for how we think, talk, and believe. Don't you have enough problems in life already? Why add to them by discouraging yourself every day with negative self-talk?

When I was a child, my favorite story was *The Little Engine that Could*. Why? Because I found it so encouraging! I used to read it over and over, and I used to think, *That's me! I think I can too!*

You need to learn to become your own encourager, your own cheerleader. Every time you do a good job, don't just let it pass; give yourself a compliment. Every time you choose discipline over indulgence, don't tell yourself that you should have anyway; recognize how much you are helping yourself. Every time you make a mistake, don't bring up everything that's wrong with yourself; tell yourself that you're paying the price for growth and that you will learn to do better next time. Every positive thing you can say to yourself will help.

2. Stop Comparing Yourself to Others

When I started my career, I looked forward to the annual report from the organization showing statistics for each of its leaders. As soon as I received them in the mail, I'd look for my standing and compare my progress with the progress of all the other leaders. After about five years of doing that, I realized how harmful it was. What happens when you compare yourself to others? Usually it's one of two things: either you perceive the other person to be far ahead of you and you feel discouraged, or you perceive yourself to be better than the other person, and you become proud. Neither of those is good for you, and neither will help you to grow.

Comparing yourself to others is really just a needless distraction. The only one you should compare yourself to is you. Your mission is to become better today than you were yesterday. You do that by focusing on what you can do today to improve and grow. Do that enough, and if you look back and compare the you of weeks, months, or years ago to the you of today, you should be greatly encouraged by your progress.

3. Move Beyond Your Limiting Beliefs

I love the old comic strip *Shoe* by Jeff MacNelly. In one of my favorites, Shoe is pitching in a baseball game. In a conference on the mound, his catcher says, "You've got to have faith in your curve ball."

"It's easy for him to say," grumbles Shoe. "When it comes to believing in myself, I'm an agnostic."

Unfortunately, that's the way a lot of people think about themselves. They don't believe that they can accomplish great things. But the greatest limitations people experience on their lives are usually the ones they impose upon themselves. As industrialist Charles Schwab said, "When a man has put a limit on what he *will* do, he has put a limit on what he *can*

> "When a man has put a limit on what he *will* do, he has put a limit on what he *can* do."
>
> —*Charles Schwab*

do." That was true for Johnnetta McSwain. As soon as she changed her self-limiting thinking, she was able to change her life.

Author Jack Canfield offers a solution to self-limiting thinking. In his book *The Success Principles*, he recommends the following four steps to transform limiting beliefs into empowering beliefs.

Identify a limiting belief that you want to change.
Determine how the belief limits you.
Decide how you want to be, act, or feel.
Create a turnaround statement that affirms or gives you permission to be, act, or feel this new way.[9]

That's really good advice. Once you do it, repeat that turnaround statement to yourself every day for as long as you must in order to change your self-limiting thinking.

For example, let's say you would like to learn a foreign language to improve your career or better enjoy a vacation, but you don't think you can do it. Once you've identified that belief, define how not learning that language is limiting you. Then describe what it will be like when you learn that language. How will it make you feel? What will it enable you to do? What might it do for your career? Then write an empowering statement that affirms your ability to learn the language, outlines the realistic process you will use to learn it, and describes how you will be impacted by this growth. Remember, in the end, it isn't what you are that holds you back; it's what you think you're not.

4. Add Value to Others

Because people with low self-esteem often see themselves as inadequate or feel like victims (which often starts because they actually have been victimized in their past), they focus inordinately on themselves. They can become self-protective and selfish because they feel that they have to be to survive.

If that is true of you, then you can combat those feelings by serving others and working to add value to them. Making a difference—even a small one—in the lives of other people lifts one's self-esteem. It's hard to feel bad about yourself when you're doing something good for someone else. In addition to that, adding value to others makes them value you more. It creates a cycle of positive feeling from one person to another.

> It's hard to feel bad about yourself when you're doing something good for someone else.

5. Do the Right Thing, Even If It's the Hard Thing

One of the best ways to build self-esteem is to do what's right. It gives a strong sense of satisfaction. And what happens whenever you don't do the right thing? Either you feel guilt, which makes you feel bad about yourself, or you lie to yourself to try to convince yourself that your actions weren't wrong or weren't that important. That does harm to you as a person and to your self-esteem.

Being true to yourself and your values is a tremendous self-esteem builder. Every time you take action that builds your character, you become stronger as a person—the harder the task, the greater the character builder. You can actually "act yourself" into feeling good about yourself, because positive character expands into every area of your life, giving you confidence and positive feelings about everything you do.

6. Practice a Small Discipline Daily in a Specific Area of Your Life

When I began my career as a minister, one of the things I did was work a little bit every day on my Sunday sermon. As I talked to my peers, I found out that this was not the way most people in my position did things. Most of my colleagues started their preparation on Friday. I couldn't understand why they would do it that way. It was like facing a mountain—overwhelming. However, I found that if I chipped away all week, by the time Friday came, I was confident that I could complete the task.

If there is an area in your life that seems overwhelming to you—health, work, family, or something else—try chipping away at it a little bit every day instead of trying to tackle it all at once. Since your self-worth is based upon the positive habits, actions, and decisions you practice every day, why not build your self-esteem and tackle your biggest problems at the same time? Don't fret or worry about it; do something specific about it. Discipline is a morale builder. Boost yours by taking small steps that will take you in a positive direction.

7. Celebrate Small Victories

This next suggestion is really a follow-up to the previous ones. When you do the right thing or you take a small step in the right direction, what is your emotional response? What kinds of things do you tell yourself? Are your thoughts like these?

Well, it's about time.
I didn't do as much as I should have.
That won't make a difference.
It's hopeless—I'll never succeed.

Or are they more like these?

It's good that I did that.
I did the right thing—good for me!
Every little bit helps.
I'm that much closer to success.

If your thinking runs more like the first list, then you need to change your thinking.

I have to admit, I have no trouble celebrating small victories. Then again, I have no trouble celebrating big victories either. I just love celebrating. You should too. Taking a break to celebrate is good for you. If nothing is ever good enough, you can lose heart. Celebrating encourages you. It helps to inspire you to keep going. Don't underestimate its power.

8. Embrace a Positive Vision for Your Life Based on What You Value

When Reese Witherspoon won the 2006 Oscar for Best Actress for her portrayal of June Carter Cash in *Walk the Line,* she quoted June Carter Cash, saying, "People used to ask June how she was doing and she would say, 'I'm just trying to matter.' I know what she means." We all want our lives to matter. That's hard to do when we don't believe *we* matter.

If you have a positive vision for your life and you take action to fulfill that vision, then you will more readily recognize that your life matters. For example, Johnnetta McSwain loved and valued her children, and she had a positive vision for them, one where they prospered and broke the cycle of violence perpetuated by the men in her family. Because of that, she took action to fulfill that vision.

What do you value? What prompts you to see a positive vision for your life? If you don't have a vision, you are likely to be apathetic. However, if you tap into what you value and try to see what could be, it can inspire you to take positive action. And every positive action you take helps you to believe in yourself, which in turn helps you to take more positive action.

9. Practice the One-Word Strategy

A couple of years ago I read a book by Kevin Hall called *Aspire*, which really inspired me. So much so that I wanted to meet the author, whom I found to be a delightful person. One of my favorite passages in the book communicates something Kevin does to help people grow:

> The first thing I do when I'm coaching some-one who aspires to stretch, grow, and go higher in life is to have that person select the one word that best describes him or her. Once that person does that, it's as if he or she has turned a page in a book and highlighted one word. Instead of see-ing three hundred different words on the page, the person's attention, and intention, is focused immediately on that single word, that single gift. What the individual focuses on expands.[10]

Why do I like this practice of picking one word? Because it tells you a lot about how you think about yourself. Try it. If you could pick only one word to describe yourself, what would it be? I hope it's

If you could pick only one word to describe yourself, what would it be?

positive! If it is, it will help you go in the right direction. If it's not, then you need to change your word.

10. Take Responsibility for Your Life

We tend to get in life what we are willing to tolerate. If we allow others to disrespect us, we get dis-
respected. If we tolerate abuse, we get abused. If we
think it's okay to be overworked and underpaid,
guess what will happen? If we don't have a plan and
purpose for our lives, we will become part of someone else's!

It's no mistake that Johnnetta McSwain's life
turned around when she took responsibility for herself and where she was, and decided to get control
of her life and make positive changes. Those changes
weren't easy, nor did they occur quickly. She had to
dig herself out of a big hole. But she did it. And so
can you.

I wish I could sit down with you, hear your story, and
encourage you specifically in your journey. If you've
had a difficult time and you don't feel good about
yourself, I want to tell you that you do have value.
You matter. Your life can change, and you can make a
difference—no matter what kind of background you
have or where you come from. No matter what trau-
mas you've suffered or mistakes you've made, you can

learn and grow. You can become the person you have the potential to be. You just need to believe in yourself to get started. And every time you take a step, think a positive thought, make a good choice, practice a small discipline, you're moving one step closer. Just keep moving forward, and keep believing.

Applying
the Law of the Mirror
to Your Life

1. Make a list of all of your best personal qualities. If you have positive self-esteem, then this will probably be easy for you. If you don't, it may be a struggle. Don't give up. If needed, spend days or weeks creating the list. Don't stop until you have written a hundred positive things about yourself.

If it took you a long time to create this list, then you need to spend time every day reading through it to remind yourself of your value. Remember, if you do not value yourself, you will have a very difficult time adding value to yourself.

Using the list as a springboard, decide on the one word that best describes you. Make this word your North Star as you begin adding value to yourself.

2. Few things impact a person's self-esteem more than the way they talk to themselves on a day-to-day basis. Are you aware of how you talk to yourself? Keep track by using your smartphone or carrying an index card so you can tally the number of times

each day this week that you think something positive or negative about yourself. In addition, you can ask close friends or family members to tell you whether they think you see yourself in a favorable or unfavorable light.

3. If you want to feel valuable, add value to others. How much time every day and every week do you spend focusing on others and adding value to them? Do you serve others through a volunteer organization? Do you mentor people? Do you give assistance to others less fortunate than yourself?

If you aren't doing so already, find a way to serve and add value to others on a weekly basis. Do something that utilizes your strengths, benefits others, and makes you feel good about yourself. Start small. If you're already serving, then do more. It's a good rule of thumb to give a tenth of your time to serving and adding value to others. So, for example, if you work forty hours a week, devote four hours to serving others.

4

The Law of Reflection

Learning to Pause Allows Growth to Catch Up with You

*"Follow effective action with quiet reflection.
From the quiet reflection will come
even more effective action."*
—PETER F. DRUCKER

There are many different ways of growing and an infinite number of lessons to be learned in life. But there are some kinds of growth that come to us *only* if we are willing to stop, pause, and allow the lesson to catch up with us. I experienced one of those in March of 2011.

A Change in Paradigm

I was traveling on an extended speaking trip, and I landed in Kiev, Ukraine, on one of my stops. While I was there, I was scheduled to speak three times to a group of about five thousand businesspeople. I had been to Kiev several times before and enjoyed both the place and the people.

About an hour before the first scheduled event, I met my Ukrainian translator. We chatted awhile so we could get to know each other. A few minutes into our conversation, he said, "I've read several of your books. You say that you want to add value to people, but that's not easy here. People don't trust leaders. And with good reason: Leaders don't add value to others here." Then he added, "I sure hope you can help them."

His words left quite an impression on me. And what he told me prompted me to recall conversations with my good friend Jim Dornan, the leader of Network 21, an organization that works in many of the countries that were once behind the Iron Curtain. Jim had told me that in any country where the government was crooked and the leaders were crooked and selfish, being able to circumvent authority and working the system were seen as virtues.

Because I still had a little time before I had to speak,

I went to the greenroom so I could pause and reflect on what I had just learned. I was feeling emotional, and I wanted to take time to let my thinking catch up to my feelings. So I started to ask myself some questions:

How was I feeling? The answer was *sad*. Living under Communist rule for generations had beaten people down, discouraged them, and made them cynical. It's hard get ahead when you have little hope.

What could I do? I could show them my heart. For some of these people, perhaps no leader had ever told them he cared about them and wanted them to succeed.

How could I do that? I could let them know that I knew what their situation was and felt for them. I could tell them that I would be just like them if I had grown up in that environment, but that there is a higher road for a leader, one where leaders add value to others. I could help them understand that even if they had never been valued by their leaders, they could become leaders who added value to others. They could become change agents for the future success of their country and themselves. I then took a moment and prayed, asking God to help me deliver that message with clarity and integrity.

I didn't completely abandon what I planned to speak about that day, but I sure modified it for and tailored it to my audience. And one of the first things

I said—which I repeated often that first day—was, "My name is John, and I'm your friend." I said it sincerely. And I also used it to help soften some hard but humorous truths I was delivering.

At first they weren't sure how to react to that statement. After a while, they started to anticipate it. By the end of the day, when I said it, they knew a zinger was coming and they'd laugh in anticipation. And the next day when I came in and prepared to speak, my translator said that everyone was saying the phrase to one another. That's when I realized that they understood that I was cheering them on and really wanted to help them.

It's never enough for me to just show up and give a good speech when I've been invited to an event. Every time I speak, I want to do two things: add value to the people I talk to and exceed the expectations of the person who invited me. It's likely I would have failed on both counts on this trip if I hadn't taken the time to pause, let the honest insights from my interpreter soak in, and change my agenda to match what my audience needed.

The Power of Pausing

If you're nearly as old as I am, you may remember an old slogan once used by Coca-Cola. They called

Coke "the pause that refreshes." That's what reflection is to someone who desires to grow. Learning to pause allows growth to catch up with you. That's the Law of Reflection.

Here are my observations concerning the power of the pause and how reflection can help you to grow:

1. Reflection Turns Experience into Insight

For over two thousand years, people have been saying that experience is the best teacher. According to one expert, the earliest recorded version of this saying came from Roman emperor Julius Caesar, who wrote, "Experience is the teacher of all things," in *De Bello Civili*.[1] With all due respect, I have to disagree with that statement. Experience is not the best teacher. Evaluated experience is! The only reason Caesar was able to make that claim was because he had learned much by reflecting on his life and writing about it.

There's an old joke that experience is a hard teacher because the test is given first and the lesson is given afterward. That's true, but only if the person takes time to reflect after the experience. Otherwise, you receive the test first and the lesson may never come. People have innumerable experiences every day, and many learn nothing from them because they never take the time to pause and reflect. That's why it is so important to pause and let understanding catch up with us.

I once heard that at the turn of the century there was a buggy whip factory that had made major improvements in their manufacturing process. They made the best-quality whips, and they were continuing to improve them. No other manufacturer in the industry compared. There was just one problem. They were working at a time when the automobile was being introduced. And it wasn't long before the entire nation would change to the horseless carriage. The company soon went out of business. I can't help wondering what the outcome might have been if the leaders of the company had taken the time to pause, understand what their experience was trying to teach them, and make changes in the course they were on.

2. Everyone Needs a Time and a Place to Pause

I have yet to meet a person who doesn't benefit from pausing and reflecting. In fact, stopping to reflect is one of the most valuable activities people can do to grow. It has much greater value to them than even motivation or encouragement. Why? Because pausing allows them to make sure they are on the right track. After all, if someone is going down the wrong road, he doesn't need motivation to speed up. He needs to stop, reflect, and change course.

In my book *Thinking for a Change*, I encourage people to identify or create a thinking place. Did I

> If someone is going down the wrong road, he doesn't need motivation to speed up. He needs to stop.

do that because there is some magic in having a designated place to pause and think? No. I did it because if you go to the trouble to create a place to pause and think and you schedule the time to go there, you will probably actually use it. And you will benefit from it.

Most people are pretty busy. There are a lot of demands on them, and they rush from place to place trying to get things done. Along the way, they have certain experiences that are *life markers*. They go to a place or are part of an event or meet a person that in some way marks them for life because something important happened. Often these markers identify for them a time of transition, change, or transformation.

If we don't take the time to pause and reflect, we can miss the significance of such events. Reflection allows those experiences to move from being life *markers* to life *makers*. If we pause to allow growth to catch up with us, it makes our lives better, because we not only better understand the significance of what we've experienced, but we can implement changes and course corrections as a result. We are also better equipped to teach others from the wisdom we have gained.

3. Pausing with Intention Expands and Enriches Thinking

Study the lives of the great people who have made an impact on the world, and you will find that in virtually every case, they spent a considerable amount of time alone thinking. Every significant religious leader in history spent time in solitude. Every political leader who had an impact on history practiced the discipline of solitude to think and plan. Great artists spend countless hours in their studios or with their instruments not just doing, but exploring their ideas and experiences. Most leading universities give their faculty time not only to teach, but to think, research, and write. Time alone allows people to sort through their experience, put it into perspective, and plan for the future.

If you are a leader, you can probably take the normal busyness of life and multiply it by ten. Leaders are so action oriented and have so many responsibilities that they are often guilty of moving all the time and neglecting to stop and take time to think. Yet this is one of the most important things leaders can do. A minute of thought is worth more than an hour of talk.

I strongly encourage you to find a place to think and to discipline yourself to pause and use it, because it has the potential to change your life. It can help

"When you are able to create a lonely place in the middle of your actions and concerns, your successes and failures slowly can lose some of their power over you."

—Henri J. M. Nouwen

you to figure out what's really important and what isn't. As writer and Catholic priest Henri J. M. Nouwen observed, "When you are able to create a lonely place in the middle of your actions and concerns, your successes and failures slowly can lose some of their power over you."

4. When You Take Time to Pause, Use Your I's

When you take the time to pause and reflect, there are really four basic directions your thinking should go:

INVESTIGATION

There's a corny old joke about two guys who have been given the job of cleaning out a stable. They're up to their ankles in horse manure, and one says to the other, "There must be a horse around here somewhere." Some things are obvious and don't require reflection to figure them out. Others require a person to play detective.

The great scientist Galileo said, "All truths are easy to understand once they are discovered. The point is to discover them. That takes investigation." Pausing means more than just slowing down to smell the roses. It means stopping and really figuring them out. That generally requires a person to ask questions, which I'll discuss in the next section of this chapter. The thing to remember is that continual growth from experiences is only possible when we discover insights and truths within them. That comes from investigation.

INCUBATION

Incubation is taking an experience of life and putting it into the slow cooker of your mind to simmer for a while. It is very similar to meditation. It's like the "flip side" of prayer. When I pray, I talk to God. When I meditate, I listen to him. Incubation is listening and learning.

I am continually putting quotes and ideas in my mental Crock-Pot to let them incubate. These days I do that by putting them in the Notes app of my iPhone. I keep them there for days, weeks, or months and look at them often to reflect on them. Here are some of the quotes I'm currently thinking about:

"If you're not at the table you're on the menu."
"You don't wait or rush yourself out of a crisis. You work yourself out."
"The mark of an effective leader is one who absorbs the punishment without surrendering his soul."

I give ideas as long as they need until I discover an insight or experience the next "I," which is...

ILLUMINATION

Jim Rohn remarked, "At the end of each day, you should play back the tapes of your performance. The results should either applaud you or prod you." What he's talking about is illumination. These are the "aha" moments in your life, the epiphanies when you experience sudden realization or insight. It's when the proverbial lightbulb turns on. Few things in life are more rewarding than such moments.

> "At the end of each day, you should play back the tapes of your performance. The results should either applaud you or prod you."
>
> —Jim Rohn

I find that I experience moments of illumination only after I spend time investigating an idea and then allowing it to incubate for a period of time. But such moments are the reward for committing time and effort to pausing and reflecting.

ILLUSTRATION

Most good ideas are like skeletons. They provide good structure, but they need meat on their bones. They lack substance, and until they have it, they aren't that useful. What would a speech be without good illustrations? A flat outline. What would a book be without fleshed-out ideas, good stories, and insightful quotes? Boring. Illustrating is the process of putting flesh on ideas.

Author and firefighter Peter M. Leschak believes, "All of us are watchers—of television, of time clocks, of traffic on the freeway—but few are observers. Everyone is looking, not many are seeing." That isn't true for people who find a place to reflect and who are intentional about pausing to allow learning to catch up with them.

Good Questions Are the Heart of Reflection

Whenever I take time to pause and reflect, I begin by asking myself a question. Whenever I'm thinking and reflecting and I feel like I have hit a roadblock, I ask myself questions. If I'm trying to learn something new or delve deeper into an area so I can grow, I ask questions. I spend a lot of my life asking questions. But that's a good thing. As author and speaker Anthony Robbins says, "Successful people ask better questions, and as a result, they get better answers."

> "Successful people ask better questions, and as a result, they get better answers."
> —*Anthony Robbins*

I cannot overemphasize the importance of asking

good questions when it comes to personal growth. If your questions are focused, they will stimulate creative thinking. Why? Because there is something about a well-worded question that often penetrates to the heart of the matter and triggers new ideas and insights. If your questions are honest, they will lead to solid convictions. If you ask quality questions, they will help you to create a high-quality life. Sir Francis Bacon—English philosopher, statesman, scientist, lawyer, jurist, author, and pioneer of the scientific method—asserted, "If a person will begin with certainties, he will end in doubts; but if he will be content to begin with doubts, he will end in certainties."

Personal Awareness Questions

Teaching other people how to ask questions effectively can be a difficult challenge because the questions they ask usually must be tailored to the situation. So perhaps the best way to give you insight on this issue is to share with you a series of questions I've asked and answered to help me develop personal awareness.

1. What Is My Biggest Asset?

I believe my greatest asset has always been my attitude. I first learned the value of a positive attitude from my father, Melvin Maxwell, who overcame his naturally pessimistic outlook by reading books by people like Norman Vincent Peale.

My wife, Margaret, also has an uncommonly good attitude. Over the years, we have occasionally wondered why others seem to have so many more problems than we do. We've finally come to the conclusion that we don't have fewer problems; we just don't allow the problems we have to get us down or distract us from what we believe is important.

What has answering this question done for me? It has not only encouraged me to continue to cultivate a positive attitude, but has also reminded me that one of the best things I can do for others is speak positively into their lives, let them know I believe in them, and encourage them in their journey.

2. What Is My Biggest Liability?

Without a doubt, having unrealistic expectations is a major shortcoming in my life. Because I am naturally optimistic, I underestimate how much time, money, and effort most endeavors will require, and that can get me into trouble.

What has answering this question done to help me grow? It has tempered my expectations toward others. Modifying my expectations to be more realistic has helped me to set up my team to succeed, rather than to fail. And it has also helped me to create more realistic goals for team members and the organizations they serve.

3. What Is My Highest High?

Without a doubt, my family is the source of the highest highs in my life. Margaret is my best friend. I cannot imagine life without her. And we are enjoying our favorite season of life now as grandparents.

4. What Is My Lowest Low?

Ironically, my lowest lows have also come as the result of family. Why? Because I love my family members so much, yet I have to let them make their own choices. That can be tough for someone with my personality. Years ago when my children were still teenagers, I was having a conversation with Ron Blue and Howie Hendricks, and I asked them, "When is this parenting thing over?" They told me it never ends. They were right.

How has it helped me to grow, knowing that the best and worst of life is related to family? It has helped me to enjoy the times I have with my family and to stay out of my grown children's decision making unless they ask for my advice.

5. What Is My Most Worthwhile Emotion?

I don't think there is a more worthwhile emotion than love. We live at our best when we love what we do, love our friends and family, even love our enemies. As a person of faith, I know this is the standard that God has set for me. It is also the desire of my heart.

How does knowing this help me to grow? Love is a choice, and it often requires effort. So to love others as I would like to do, I must be intentional about it and choose to love people every day.

6. What Is My Least Worthwhile Emotion?

The least attractive emotion not only for me, but for any person, is self-pity. It is destructive and self-serving. In *Earth & Altar,* Eugene H. Peterson says,

> Pity is one of the noblest emotions available to human beings; self-pity is possibly the most ignoble. Pity is the capacity to enter into the pain of another in order to do something about it; self-pity is an incapacity, a crippling emotional disease that severely distorts our perception of reality. Pity discovers the need in others for love and healing and then fashions speech

and action that bring strength; self-pity reduces the universe to a personal wound that is displayed as proof of significance. Pity is adrenaline for acts of mercy; self-pity is a narcotic that leaves its addicts wasted and derelict.

Knowing the negative effects of self-pity reminds me to avoid it categorically. It cannot help me, and it will always harm me.

7. What Is My Best Habit?

H. P. Liddon, chancellor of St. Paul's in London in the 1800s, observed, "What we do on some great occasion will depend on what we are; and what we are will be the result of previous years of self-discipline." I believe that a hundred percent. That is one of the reasons I work hard to follow through on daily disciplines. I believe a person's secret of success is found in his daily agenda.

> "What we do on some great occasion will depend on what we are; and what we are will be the result of previous years of self-discipline."
>
> —H. P. Liddon

Perhaps the greatest value of questioning myself in this area is that it exposes my weakness regarding the discipline for my health. Developing good eating habits has been a lifelong struggle. And I did not exercise regularly until after I suffered my heart attack. I continue to work hard to try to grow in this area.

8. What Is My Worst Habit?

Without a doubt, my worst personal trait is impatience. It was part of my early nature as a child, and it has become ingrained in me as a habit. When I was a child, we used to visit my grandpa Maxwell, and it never failed that at some point while we were there, he would sit my

> There are things in life that you have to work for and there are things you have to wait for.

brother, Larry, and me down in two chairs and offer to pay us a nickel if we would sit quietly in those chairs for five minutes. Larry *always* earned his nickel. And I *never* did—not one time!

I have learned that there are things in life that you have to work for and there are things you have to wait for. I'm still trying to grow when it comes to waiting. I suspect that this will be a goal of mine until the day I die.

9. What Is Most Fulfilling to Me?

The thing I enjoy doing most is communicating to other people. When I communicate, I know I am in my strength zone, I feel the most fulfilled, and I make the greatest impact. Every time I do it, I have a sense deep down that says, *I was made for this.*

Early in my career, knowing that communication was fulfilling to me prompted me to become a better speaker, because back then I wasn't very good at it. For more than ten years, it was one of the top areas I dedicated myself to when it came to growth. I continue to try to grow as a communicator, but the value I receive from asking this question today is that it helps me to stay focused so I'm doing what returns the most value to others and to myself.

10. What Do I Prize Most Highly?

I value nothing as highly as I do my faith. It forms my values. It guides my actions. It has been the foundation of my teaching on leadership. It is my source and my security. Mother Teresa said, "Faith keeps the person who keeps the faith." I have found that to be true.

> Faith is "trusting in advance what will only make sense in reverse."
>
> —Philip Yancey

Author Philip Yancey described faith as "trusting in advance what will only make sense in reverse." Having faith and knowing its value in my life helps me to have a divine perspective every day. I need that because I can easily get off course otherwise.

The previous ten questions were ones I actually asked myself to prompt me to reflect and help me grow in the area of self-awareness. You can ask yourself questions in just about any area of life to help you pause, focus, and learn. For example, if you wanted to grow in the area of relationships, you could ask yourself the following questions:

1. Do I value people?
2. Do people know I value them?
3. How do I show it?
4. Am I a "plus" or a "minus" in my most important relationships?
5. What evidence do I have to confirm my opinion?
6. What is the love language of the people I love?
7. How can I serve them?
8. Do I need to forgive someone in my life who needs to be given grace?
9. Who in my life should I take time to thank?
10. Who in my life should be receiving more of my time?

Or if you wanted to pause and think about where you are in the area of personal growth, you could ask yourself the following:

1. Do I know and practice the 15 Laws of Personal Growth?
2. Which three laws do I do best?
3. Which three are my weakest?
4. Am I growing daily?
5. What am I doing daily to grow?
6. How am I growing?
7. What are the roadblocks that are keeping me from growing?
8. What are the breakthroughs I need to keep growing?
9. What were the potential learning moments I experienced today, and did I seize them?
10. Am I passing on to someone what I am learning?

What you want to accomplish in life and where you are in the journey will determine what areas you most need to think about today, tailoring the questions to yourself. But the most important thing you must do is write out the questions and write out the answers. Why? Because you will discover that what you think after you write the answer is different from what you thought before you wrote it. Writing helps you to discover what you truly know, think, and believe.

Worth the Trouble

All of this probably sounds like a lot of steps and a lot of trouble. You're right; it is. That's why most people never do it. But it is worth every bit of effort you put into it. The farther you go in life, the more critical it is that you take time to pause and think. The older you are, the less time you have to stay on purpose and do the things you were created to do. But here's the good news: If you've been diligent in your efforts to grow along the way, you will also be better equipped to fulfill that purpose, even if it requires you to make significant changes or course corrections.

Many years ago my friend Bob Buford wrote a book called *The Second Half.* It's fantastic. The entire book is a "pause so that growth can catch up with you" experience. In it, he encourages readers who've experienced some success in the first half of their lives to stop and think about what they want to do in the second half. Here is some of the advice he gives:

> You will not get very far in your second half without knowing your life mission. Can yours be stated in a sentence or two? A good way to begin formulating one is with some questions (and nakedly honest answers). What is your

passion? What have you achieved? What have you done uncommonly well? How are you wired? Where do you belong? What are the "shoulds" that have trailed you during the first half? These and other questions like them will direct you toward the self your heart longs for; they will help you discover the tasks for which you were especially made.

Never forget that your goal in personal growth is reaching your potential. To do that, you need to keep pausing, keep asking questions, and keep growing every day.

Applying the Law of Reflection to Your Life

1. Have you created a place where you can consistently and effectively pause and reflect? If not, do so immediately. First, figure out what kind of environment will be good for you. Among the places I have chosen over the years are a rock outdoors, a small isolated room where no one would bother me, and a special chair in my office. Figure out what works for you, and stick with it for as long as it's effective.

2. Schedule time to pause and reflect. If you don't, it will always get shuffled off of your to-do list. Ideally, you would spend a short time pausing to reflect at the end of every day (between ten and thirty minutes), a significant time every week (at least an hour or two), part of a day several times a year (half a day), and an extended time annually (as little as a day and as much as a week). Put these times to pause on your calendar and guard them as you would your most important appointments.

3. Cartoonist Henri Arnold said, "The wise man questions himself, the fool others." The Law of Reflection will do you little good unless you are intentional in your thinking time. You make yourself intentional by asking yourself tough questions.

> "The wise man questions himself, the fool others."
> —Henri Arnold

Where do you most need to grow right now? Is it in self-management? Is there an issue that you can't seem to wrestle down? Are you experiencing a plateau in your career? Are you failing to win at the most important relationships in your life? Do you need to examine or reexamine your purpose? Do you need to assess what you should be doing in your second half?

Whatever your issue is, create questions around it and spend time writing your answer to those questions during your scheduled times of reflection.

5

The Law of Consistency

Motivation Gets You Going—Discipline Keeps You Growing

"The hallmark of excellence, the test of greatness, is consistency."

—Jim Tressel

When I started my speaking career, I believed that motivating people was the key to helping them succeed. *If I can get them moving in the right direction,* I thought, *they will be successful.* I would do my best to give people reasons to work hard. I'd try to make them laugh. I'd try to touch their hearts. My goal was to inspire people so much that they'd be ready to charge hell with a water pistol. When I was done, I'd walk away thinking I'd done a good job. But often whatever motivation people received didn't seem to last very long.

I'm still a big believer in motivation. Everyone wants to be encouraged. Everyone enjoys being inspired. But here's the truth when it comes to personal growth: Motivation gets you going, but discipline keeps you growing. That's the Law of Consistency. It doesn't matter how talented you are. It doesn't matter how many opportunities you receive. If you want to grow, consistency is key.

How to Grow in Consistency

If you want to become more disciplined and consistent in your performance, you need to become more disciplined and consistent in your growth. How can you do that? By knowing the what, how, why, and when of personal improvement. Take some time to consider the following four questions about your growth:

1. Do You Know What You Need to Improve?

Journalist and author George Lorimer remarked, "You've got to get up every morning with determination if you're going to go to bed with satisfaction." That's true, but it's important to know where to direct that determination.

I've already discussed this in some detail, but I think it bears repeating. You must develop yourself to be successful. All the time I see people with purpose who are inconsistent in their progress. They have the ambition to succeed and they show aptitude for their job, yet they do not move forward. Why? Because they think they can master their job and don't need to master themselves. What a mistake. Your future is dependent upon your personal growth. Improving yourself daily guarantees you a future filled with possibilities. When you expand yourself, you expand your horizons, your options, your opportunities, your potential.

> "You've got to get up every morning with determination if you're going to go to bed with satisfaction."
> —George Lorimer

From the start of my career in 1969, if I had spent all my time perfecting my ability to do my job, I never would have grown. But because I focused on improving myself, I grew from taking care of people to leading them. I went from speaking to audiences to writing books. I expanded from influencing only small religious organizations to many different kinds of organizations. I improved my focus from institutional to entrepreneurial. My influence changed from local to national to international. I went from maintaining organizations to founding and growing them. Why has this happened to me? Because *what*

I did was try to improve myself, not just my job or position. It opened up my future. It has allowed me to achieve much more than I ever believed I would be capable of doing.

E. M. Gray said, "The successful person has the habit of doing the things that failures don't like to do. The successful person doesn't like doing them either, but his dislike is subordinated to the strength of his purpose." The more tuned in you are to your purpose, and the more dedicated you are to growing toward it, the better your chances of reaching your potential, expanding your possibilities, and doing something significant.

2. Do You Know How You Are Supposed to Improve?

The question of *how* to improve is one of the main reasons I started to work hard at changing from being a motivational speaker to becoming a motivational teacher. I didn't want people to walk away from one of my teaching sessions inspired but uncertain how to proceed. To grow, most people need knowledge, experience, and coaching.

Do you have a handle on how to improve yourself? I have four very simple suggestions that can get you started:

MATCH YOUR MOTIVATION TO YOUR PERSONALITY TYPE

Not everyone gets motivated the same way or is motivated by the same things. To give yourself a fighting chance to become consistent in your growth, start by leveraging your personality type to get yourself going. There are dozens of personality profiles and systems that people use. I like the one based on the classic personality types that has been taught by Florence Littauer.

The first type of person is *phlegmatic*. The strength of people with this personality is that they are easygoing and likeable. Their weakness is inertia. If you're phlegmatic, how can you motivate yourself? By finding the value in what you need to do. When phlegmatics see the value in doing something, they can be one of the most tenacious (meaning stubborn) of all personality types.

At the opposite end of the personality spectrum from phlegmatics are *cholerics*. The strength of people with this personality type is that they take charge easily and make decisions quickly. Their weakness is that if they are not "in charge," they refuse to participate. If you are choleric, how can you tap into internal motivation? By focusing on the choices you can make. Every person is in charge of his own growth. Choose how you will grow and stick with it.

The most fun-loving of all the personality types are people who are *sanguine*. They are often the life of every party. Their weakness is often lack of focus. If you're sanguine, how can you motivate yourself to grow? By making a game of it. If that seems impossible, then give yourself rewards for incremental successes.

The final personality type is *melancholic*. These are life's perfectionists. Attention to detail is their strength. But because they desire to do everything perfectly, they are afraid of making mistakes. If you are melancholic, how do you motivate yourself beyond that fear? By focusing on the joy of learning details and the potential for developing a level of mastery over your subject matter.

As you can see, every personality type has its strengths. You just need to tap that strength in your personality to set yourself up for success when it comes to motivation.

START WITH THE SIMPLE STUFF

What is the number one mistake of first-time gardeners? The same as that of many people who approach personal growth for the first time: attempting too much. What is the result? Discouragement.

When you attempt too much too soon, you're almost guaranteed to fall short of your desired results. That is demotivating. The secret to building motivational momentum is to start small with the simple stuff.

A humorous take on this thought was captured in the comic strip *Peanuts* by Charles Schulz. After striking out on the baseball field—as usual—Charlie Brown returns to the dugout and slumps down on the bench.

"Rats!" he laments. "I'll never be a big-league player. I just don't have it! All my life I've dreamed of playing in the big leagues, but I know I'll never make it."

Lucy, ever one to give advice, replies, "Charlie Brown, you're thinking too far ahead. What you need to do is set more immediate goals for yourself."

"Immediate goals?" Charlie asks. Like many people, he has never considered such a thing.

"Yes," Lucy advises, "start with the next inning. When you go out to pitch, see if you can walk out to the mound without falling down!"

Industrialist Ian MacGregor observed, "I work on the same principle as people who train horses. You start with low fences, easily achieved goals, and work up. It's important in management never to ask people to try to accomplish goals they can't accept."

If you want to gain momentum and improve your motivation, begin by setting goals that are worthwhile but highly achievable. Master the basics. Then practice them every day without fail. Small disciplines repeated with consistency every day lead to great achievements gained slowly over time. This is an especially good idea to implement when reading a book. In fact, when I wrote *25 Ways to Win with People*, I suggested that readers working on their people skills practice one of twenty-five skills each week. It creates an easy way to make progress doing something simple day by day.

If you want to grow, don't try to win big. Try to win small. Andrew Wood asserted, "Where many people go wrong in trying to reach their goals is in constantly looking for the big hit, the home run, the magic answer that suddenly transforms their dreams into reality. The problem is that the big hit never comes without a great deal of little hits first. Success in most things comes not from some gigantic stroke of fate, but from simple, incremental progress."

> Small disciplines repeated with consistency every day lead to great achievements gained slowly over time.

BE PATIENT

When I give the advice to be patient, I am the person who most needs to take it. As I mentioned in the last chapter, impatience is one of my greatest weaknesses. I think it comes from having unrealistic expectations—for myself and others. Everything I want to do takes longer than I anticipate. Every endeavor I lead is more difficult than I believed it would be. Every project I attempt costs more than I expected. Every task I hand off to another person is more complicated than I hoped. Some days I believe that patience is a minor form of despair disguised as a virtue.

I'm not alone in this. If you're an American, as I am, you may agree that as a culture, we have a problem with patience. We want everything fast. We live in a country with fast-food restaurants and fast-weight-loss clinics. How ironic.

Persian poet Saadi instructed, "Have patience. All things are difficult before they become easy." That's wise advice. Most people never realize how close they are to achieving significant things, because they give up too soon. Everything worthwhile in life takes dedication and time. The people who grow and achieve the most are the ones who harness the power of patience and persistence.

> "Have patience.
> All things are
> difficult before they
> become easy."
> —*Saadi*

VALUE THE PROCESS

One of the best things you can do for yourself as a learner is to cultivate the ability to value and enjoy the process of growth. It is going to take a long time, so you might as well enjoy the journey.

Several years ago I was having dinner with my friends Vern and Charlene Armitage. Charlene is a successful life coach who works with many clients. I asked what she focused on when coaching. Her answer highlighted the importance of the process that people must develop in order to grow and change the direction of their lives. She said, "Life goals are reached by setting annual goals. Annual goals are reached by reaching daily goals. Daily goals are reached by doing things which may be uncomfortable at first but eventually become habits. Habits are powerful things. Habits turn actions into attitudes, and attitudes into lifestyles."

You can visualize tomorrow using it as motivation to grow, but if you want to actually grow, your focus needs to be on today. If you value today and find a way to enjoy it, you will invest in today. And the small steps you take today will lead to the bigger steps you take someday.

In their book *Winning: The Answers*, Jack and Suzy Welch assert, "Too many people believe that one big, public success will solve their self-confidence problems forever. That only happens in the movies. In real life, the opposite strategy is what works. Call it the 'small victories' approach." They go on to describe Jack's first experience as a speaker. Even with detailed notes and lots of practice, the fifteen-minute effort was a disaster. So he made it his goal to improve incrementally, which he accomplished by valuing the process. Instead of letting fear or failures overwhelm him, he stared defeat in the face, figured out what went wrong, set a new goal, and started again. They explain, "In time, you will discover that all failing really does teach you something you needed to know—so you can regroup and stretch again, with ever more...nerve." That strategy has paid off. "Today," they write, "answering questions without notes in front of thousands of people is the opposite of nerve-racking; it's fun."[1] That kind of progress cannot happen if you don't value the process.

3. Do You Know Why You Want to Keep Improving?

Knowing *what* to improve and *how* to improve are critical to consistency in personal growth. But so is knowing *why*. The *how* and *what* will take you only so far. The why is what keeps you motivated long after that first rush of energy and enthusiasm wears off. It can carry you through when willpower isn't enough. Think of it as why-power.

I love the story of the salesman who looked out the window of the hotel restaurant at a blinding snowstorm. He asked his waiter, "Do you think the roads will be clear enough in the morning to travel?"

The waiter replied, "Depends on if you're on salary or commission."

Having a strong *why* will help you to keep going when the discipline of learning becomes difficult, discouraging, or tedious. If your growth is connected to your values, dreams, and purpose, you'll know why you're doing it. And you will be more likely to follow through.

One of the ways to judge whether you have tapped into your *why*s is to take what my friend Mike Murdock calls "The Why Test." Your answers to the following seven questions will let you know if your *why* is solid enough to motivate you to consistently grow:

Question 1: Do you constantly procrastinate on important tasks?

Question 2: Do you require coaxing to do small chores?

Question 3: Do you perform duties just to get by?

Question 4: Do you constantly talk negatively about your work?

Question 5: Do efforts of friends to encourage you irritate you instead?

Question 6: Do you start small projects and abandon them?

Question 7: Do you avoid self-improvement opportunities?

If you answer yes to many of these questions, you haven't tapped into a strong enough or big enough *why* to keep you growing.

When I was a child, my mom continually gave me *why*s to keep me going. She would say things like, "If you eat your vegetables, you can have dessert." She knew I needed to know the benefits of eating vegetables when I didn't want to do it. That kind of training set me up for success, because I started to learn the relationship between motivation and discipline. If you think about it, you can see that discipline and motivation are two sides of the same coin. If you have the motivation you need, discipline is no problem. If you lack motivation, discipline is always a problem.

> "Once you learn to quit it becomes a habit."
>
> —*Vince Lombardi*

You have to give yourself more and bigger *why*s so you can keep *wanting* to put in the effort to grow. In my book *Put Your Dream to the Test*, I teach that the more valid reasons you have to achieve your dream, the higher the odds are that you will. That principle is also true of growth. The greater number of reasons you give yourself to grow, the more likely you will be to follow through. Of course, in certain circumstances one really compelling *why* can also be enough, as Kenyan world-class runner Bernard "Kip" Lagat demonstrated when he was interviewed during the Sydney Olympics. He was asked how his country was able to produce so many great distance runners. His answer: "It's the road signs: 'Beware the Lions.'"[2]

Legendary NFL coach Vince Lombardi said, "Once you learn to quit it becomes a habit." If giving up has become a habit for you, then I suggest you take the advice of my friend Darren Hardy, who wrote a wonderful book called *The Compound Effect*. In it he writes,

The Compound Effect is the principle of reaping huge rewards from a series of small, smart choices. What's most interesting about this process to me is that, even though the results are massive, the steps, in the moment, don't *feel* significant. Whether you're using this strategy for improving your health, relationships, finances, or anything else for that matter, the changes are so subtle, they're almost imperceptible. These small changes offer little or no immediate result, no big win, no obvious I-told-you-so payoff. So why bother?

Most people get tripped up by the simplicity of the Compound Effect. For instance, they quit after the eighth day of running because they're still overweight. Or, they stop practicing the piano after six months because they haven't mastered anything other than "Chopsticks." Or, they stop making contributions to their IRA after a few years because they could use the cash—and it doesn't seem to be adding up to much anyway.

What they don't realize is that these small, seemingly insignificant steps completed consistently over time will create a radical difference.[3]

When you make the right choices—however small—and do it consistently over time, it can make a huge difference in your life. If you remember *why* you're making those choices, it becomes easier.

4. Do You Know When You Are Supposed to Improve?

The final piece of the puzzle is the question of *when*. When do you need to improve? First the obvious answer: right now. Today. Author and education professor Leo Buscaglia noted, "Life lived for tomorrow will always be just a day away from being realized." So you need to get started if you haven't yet. More important, you need today to be every day.

You will never change your life until you change something you do daily. That means developing great habits. Discipline is the bridge between goals and accomplishments, and that bridge must be crossed every day. Over time that daily crossing becomes a habit. And ultimately, people do not decide their future; they decide their habits and their habits decide their future. As author and speaker Brian Tracy says, "From the time you get up in the morning to the time you go to sleep at night, your habits largely control the words you say, the things you do, and the ways you react and respond."

> You will never change your life until you change something you do daily.

What are you doing daily that needs to change? What needs doing? Maybe more important, what needs undoing? Advice columnist Abigail Van Buren quipped, "A bad habit never goes away by itself. It's always an undo-it-yourself project." What are you willing to change doing today in order to change what you will be doing tomorrow?

In the end, hard work is really the accumulation of easy things you didn't do when you should have. It's like diet and exercise. Everyone wants to be thin, but no one wants to make the right choices to get there. It's hard work when you've neither eaten right nor exercised day after day. However, if you make small right choices each day, day after day, you see results.

Maybe It's Time to Stop Setting Goals

Consistency isn't easy. Novelist Aldous Huxley asserted, "Consistency is contrary to nature, contrary to life. The only completely consistent people are the dead." Even so, to be successful we must learn to become consistent. You must figure out what works for you, but I'll be glad to tell you what has worked for me. Instead of being goal conscious, I focus on being growth conscious. Here's the difference:

GOAL CONSCIOUSNESS	GROWTH CONSCIOUSNESS
Focuses on a destination	Focuses on the journey
Motivates you and others	Matures you and others
Seasonal	Lifelong
Challenges you	Changes you
Stops when a goal is reached	Keeps you growing beyond the goal

I am such a strong believer in people and in human potential—not only in others but also myself—that I don't ever want to put a lid on it by setting goals that are too small. I did that early in my career, and I realized it would limit me. If you can believe in yourself and the potential that is in you, and then focus on growth instead of goals, there's no telling how far you can grow. You just need to consistently put in the work as you keep believing in yourself.

Consistently Productive

Author Ernest Newman noted, "The great composer does not set to work because he is inspired, but becomes inspired because he is working. Beethoven, Wagner, Mozart, and Bach all settled down, day after day, to the job at hand. They didn't waste time waiting for inspiration." That has also been true of one of today's most famous and productive composers: John Williams. No doubt you know the man's work, even if you don't know his name. Do you remember the five musical notes that were the communication key in the movie *Close Encounters of the Third Kind*? Or the ominous music that always accompanied the appearance of the shark in *Jaws*? How about the themes from *Star Wars* or *Raiders of the Lost Ark* or the *Harry Potter* films? All of those were John Williams's compositions.

Williams, the son of a jazz

> "The great composer does not set to work because he is inspired, but becomes inspired because he is working."
>
> —Ernest Newman

musician, was born in Queens, New York, and grew up in Los Angeles. He showed musical promise early and studied with Italian composer Mario Castelnuovo-Tedesco. After a stint serving in the U.S. Air Force, he studied piano at Juilliard, then played at clubs and studios in New York City. He broke into the movie industry by working for composers such as Franz Waxman, Bernard Herrmann, Alfred Newman, Henry Mancini, and Jerry Goldsmith playing piano, scoring, and eventually composing. His first screen credit came in 1960.[4]

Williams has been working steadily in the movies for more than sixty years. In that time, he has written 121 film scores, a symphony, a dozen concertos, and many other symphonic works. He has been nominated for Academy Awards forty-five times, winning five times. He's been awarded four Golden Globes, five Emmys, and twenty-one Grammys.[5] And he's still going strong. How does he do it? By being consistent. Williams says,

I developed from very early on a habit of writing something every day, good or bad. There are good days, and there are less good days, but I do a certain amount of pages it seems to me before I can feel like the day has been completely served. When I am working on a film, of course, it's a six-day-a-week affair, and when I'm not working on films, I always like to devote myself to some piece, some musical project, that gives me a feeling that I'm maybe contributing in some small way or, maybe more importantly, learning in the process.[6]

Williams doesn't look for motivation. He doesn't wait for inspiration. He gets up every morning and practices the discipline of writing. He doesn't expect it to be perfect. He just expects it to be done.

And what about writer's block? Williams says it's not a problem:

I never experienced anything like a block. For me if I'm ever blocked or I feel like I don't quite know where to go at the next turn, the best thing for me is to keep writing, to write something. It could be absolute nonsense, but it will project me into the next phase of thinking. And I think if we ourselves as writers get out of the way and let the flow happen and not get uptight about it, so to speak, the muses will carry us along.

The wonderful thing about music is it never seems to be exhausted. Every little idea germinates another one. Things are constantly transforming themselves in musical terms. So that the few notes we have, 7, 8 or 12 notes, can be morphed into endless variations, and it's never quite over, so I think the idea of a block is something we need to work through.[7]

John Williams's life and work is proof that the Law of Consistency can work. Anyone who does what he must only when he is in the mood or when it's convenient isn't going to be successful. The secret is following through. Williams's body of work is the evidence of a lifetime of self-discipline and perseverance. And it verifies what SuccessNet founder Michael Angier says: "If you develop the habits of success, you'll make success a habit."

> "If you develop the habits of success, you'll make success a habit."
> —Michael Angier

That habit of success hasn't gone to Williams's head. "If the music is well known," he says, "it speaks to the ubiquitous nature of film in our society. With time I suppose everything, all but the greatest works of art, are erased from memory, but I feel lucky and very privileged that people respond in the way that they do."[8]

I find John Williams's music and his life very inspiring. I hope you do too. But never forget: Motivation gets you going, but discipline keeps you growing. That is the Law of Consistency.

Applying
the Law of Consistency
to Your Life

1. Align your methods of motivation with your personality type. Use whatever personality profile you prefer to study your personality type. (If you haven't used one before, then find one. Examples include Myers-Briggs Type Indicator, DiSC, and Personality Plus.) Once you have a good handle on what makes your personality type tick, then develop a daily growth system that is simple and plays to your strengths.

2. It's difficult to remain engaged in anything if you have not found a way to value and appreciate the process. Make a list of everything you like about personal growth. If your list is very short, really work at it. *Anything* you can find as motivation will help you to develop better growth habits.

3. The more *whys* you have for pursuing personal growth on a daily basis, the more likely you will

be to follow through. Start compiling those *why*s. Think of immediate benefits as well as long-term ones. Consider reasons related to purpose, vision, and dreams. Think of how it will help you relationally, vocationally, and spiritually. Any reason to grow is a good reason as long as it's *your* reason.

6

The Law of Environment

Growth Thrives in Conducive Surroundings

"The first step toward success is taken when you refuse to be a captive of the environment you first find yourself in."
—Mark Caine

I believe at some point during every person's lifetime, there comes a need to change environments in order to grow. That may seem obvious in the case of someone like Johnnetta McSwain, whom I wrote about in the Law of the Mirror chapter. She grew up in a terrible situation and suffered horrible abuse. But I also believe it's true even for people who grow up in positive, nurturing environments. If we want to grow to reach our potential, we must be in the right environment. That usually requires us to make changes in our life.

Time for a Change

I grew up in a great home environment. I had two loving parents. My father led our family proactively, helping each of us three kids find our purpose and develop our talents. My mother loved us unconditionally (and believe me, there were days when I know I was a challenge, because I didn't like rules and was always pushing the boundaries). I had lots of friends. I received a good education. I headed off to a career I loved after marrying my high school sweetheart. What could be better?

But less than ten years into my career, I realized that the environment I was in wasn't conducive to reaching my full potential. In my late twenties, I was already being considered to lead the premier church in the denomination. I wanted to learn a lot more, and by their grooming me for that position so early in my career, I felt like they were saying that I was at the top of the class. What's the problem with that? If you're always at the head of the class, then you're in the wrong class. The best place to learn is always where others are ahead of you.

If you're always at the head of the class, then you're in the wrong class.

Just to set the record straight, so you don't think

I'm bragging, I need to tell you that I was a medium-sized fish in a *very* small pond. I wasn't as good as they were giving me credit for. The people in my denomination were good people. I admired the character and integrity of many of their leaders. So that wasn't the problem. I just knew I needed more room to grow. To do that, I would have to change environments.

I went to my father, a lifelong pastor in that organization, who had been a college president and an executive in the denomination's leadership, and talked with him about the issue. He agreed that I needed to move on into a larger pond so I could grow more easily. That took understanding and courage on his part, because after I left, he would remain in the organization, and he would endure a lot of criticism from others in the organization for my move. But he did it with grace, and he always supported my decision. And I feel certain that had I remained where I was, I would not have grown the way I have, nor would I have come as far.

Change Depends on Your Choices

You've probably seen the phrase *growth = change.* It's possible to change without growing, but it's impossible to grow without changing. One of the keys to making the right changes that allow us to grow is knowing the difference between a problem or challenge, which I can change, and a fact of life, which I cannot. For example, one day as a teenager I looked into the mirror and came to a sudden realization. I was not a handsome guy. It was a fact of life. I couldn't change my face. What was I going to do? I made a decision. I would change my attitude about it. I would smile. Did it change my face? No, not really. But it helped me to look better.

Like me, you must deal with many facts of life. You cannot change where and when you were born. You cannot change who your parents are. You cannot change your height or your DNA. But you can change your attitude about them. You must do your best to live with them.

A problem is different. A problem is something you *can* do something about. It's something you can *grow* through. How? Ironically, it begins with a similar first step: a change in attitude. When you change your attitude regarding a problem, you open up many opportunities for growth.

> "Whether you are a success or failure in life has little to do with your circumstances; it has much more to do with your choices."
>
> —*Nido Qubein*

Businessman, author, and speaker Nido Qubein asserted, "Whether you are a success or failure in life has little to do with your circumstances; it has much more to do with your choices." What choices do you need to make so you are in conducive surroundings where you will thrive and grow? When it comes to environment, I believe we need to make the following six choices to put ourselves in a better place for growth:

1. Assess Your Current Environment

Professor and preacher Ernest Campbell tells a story about a lonely woman who purchased a parrot from a pet store. After only one day of having it, she returned to the store and told the storekeeper how disappointed she was with it. "That parrot hasn't said a word yet!" she lamented.

"Does it have a mirror?" asked the storekeeper. "Parrots like to be able to look at themselves in the mirror." So the lady bought a mirror and returned home.

The next day she was back again, reporting that the bird still wasn't speaking. "What about a ladder?" the storekeeper asked. "Parrots enjoy walking up and down a ladder." So the parrot owner bought a ladder and returned home.

On the third day, she was back again with the same complaint. "Does the parrot have a swing?" was the shopkeeper's solution. "Birds enjoy relaxing on a swing." She bought the swing and went home.

The next day she returned to the store and

announced that the bird had died. "I'm terribly sorry to hear that," said the storekeeper. "Did the bird ever say anything before it died?"

"Yes," said the lady. "It said, 'Don't they sell any food down there?'"

What's the moral of this silly story? Change just for the sake of change is not going to help you. If you are going to make changes, you must make sure they're the right ones. How do you do that? Start by assessing where you are now and why you want to change.

When I was considering making the transition from one professional environment to another, I spent a good amount of time examining why I wanted to change. For me, there were three main reasons to make the transition:

- I had gone to the top too fast.
- I did not feel challenged enough.
- There was nowhere else I wanted to go in the organization.

Those factors were enough to make me look at the uncomfortable truth of needing to make changes to where I was and what I was doing.

One of the ways to judge whether you're growing and in a conducive growth environment is to discern whether you're looking forward to what you're doing or looking back at what you've done. If the future looks dull, routine, or confining, you may need to start looking to make changes.

Like me, you may be able to intuitively sense if you are not in the kind of environment that is going to promote your growth. However, if you find it difficult to make that judgment about your situation, then you can approach it from another direction. You can ask yourself questions to help you understand who and what nurtures you personally, and then figure out whether or not you're getting those things. Here's a list of questions to help you get started:

Music—What songs lift me?
Thoughts—What ideas speak to me?
Experiences—What experiences rejuvenate me?
Friends—What people encourage me?
Recreation—What activities revive me?
Soul—What spiritual exercises strengthen me?
Hopes—What dreams inspire me?
Home—What family members care for me?
Giftedness—What blessings activate me?
Memories—What recollections make me smile?
Books—What have I read that changed me?

You get the idea. I'm sure you will be able to add other categories and questions to help you understand what encourages you to grow. The main idea is to know yourself and to assess whether you're getting what you need in your current environment. If you are, celebrate. If you're not, prepare yourself to make some hard choices.

2. Change Yourself and Your Environment

If you know that you need to make a major change to your environment, then there's something you must keep in mind: You must also determine to change yourself at the same time. Here's why: If you try to...

Change yourself but not your environment—growth will be slow and difficult;

Change your environment but not yourself—growth will be slow and less difficult;

Change your environment *and* yourself—growth will be faster and more successful.

By putting both together at the same time, you increase and accelerate your chances for success.

When I first realized I needed to grow—after the encounter with Curt Kampmeier that I recounted in the Law of Intentionality—I found it difficult to actually do. Few people shared my enthusiasm for growth. I had few models. Most of the people around me in my little world were content to work hard and merely make a living. I wanted more than that. I wanted to make an impact. During that time I remember sitting down and thinking about what a growth environment would look like. Over the course of many weeks, I penned what I call "My Growth Environment." It has helped to guide my decision making concerning personal growth since I wrote it in 1973. It says, in a growth environment...

> Others are *Ahead* of me.
> I am continually *Challenged*.
> My focus is *Forward*.
> The atmosphere is *Affirming*.
> I am often out of my *Comfort Zone*.
> I wake up *Excited*.
> Failure is not my *Enemy*.
> Others are *Growing*.
> People desire *Change*.
> Growth is *Modeled* and *Expected*.

When my intuition was telling me that my environment wasn't conducive to personal growth, I went back to that list and found that most of those statements did not apply to my current situation. So I determined to change myself and change my environment. If you read that list and you sensed that most of those statements did not apply to your life, then you may need to do the same thing.

I learned a lot about changing myself in 1975 when I attended a conference in Waterloo, Iowa. At that conference I saw Charles "Tremendous" Jones for the first time. It was there that I also met an author whose books I admired: Elmer Towns. I was surprised but delighted when he invited me to sit next to him on a flight to Chicago on our way home so we could talk. During our conversation, he taught me the Hot Poker Principle. "Do you know how to get a poker hot?" Elmer asked me. "Put it next to the fire." He then went on to explain that we're like the metal in a poker. If our environment is cold, we're cold. If it's hot, we're hot. "If you want to grow," he said, "then spend time with great people; visit great places; attend great events; read great books, listen to great tapes." Those words sent me on my quest to meet with leaders around the country who were ahead of me professionally. It changed my life.

As you consider changing yourself and your environment, think about the elements that the right kind of growth environment provide:

The right *soil* to grow in: What nourishes me? Growth.

The right *air* to breathe in: What keeps me alive?
   Purpose.
The right *climate* to live in: What sustains me?
   People.

They say that if you put a pumpkin in a jug when it's the size of a walnut, it will grow to the size and shape of the jug and never get bigger. That can happen to a person's thinking. Don't allow that to happen to you.

3. Change Who You Spend Your Time With

Early in my life I learned the importance of a right environment and who I spent my time with. My parents were very wise in this area. Though my parents never had a lot of money when we were growing up, they created the kind of home environment where all of our friends wanted to come and spend time. My dad made a basketball court by pouring a concrete pad and putting up a basketball hoop. They fitted out our basement as a kid's paradise, complete with a pool table, Ping-Pong table, and chemistry set. We had few reasons to hang out anywhere but home, and our friends had every reason to come over. And my mother was always around, getting to know all the kids. She influenced all the friends she could, and warned us about the behavior of those who might lead us into trouble. She and my dad understood that birds of a feather flock together. And their efforts paid off. Kids flowed to our house. Even today— more than five decades later—whenever I see any of the people I grew up with, they still talk about coming over to my house as a kid and hanging out in our "basement canteen." It was a destination.

According to research by social psychologist Dr. David McClelland of Harvard, the people with whom you habitually associate are called your "reference group," and these people determine as much as 95 percent of your success or failure in life.

Many people have given their take on this truth. King Solomon of Israel wrote, "Walk with the wise and become wise, for a companion of fools suffers harm."[1] Charles "Tremendous" Jones is well known for saying, "You are the same today that you are going to be in five years from now except for two things: the people with whom you associate and the books you read." And Jim Rohn asserted that we become the combined average of the five people we hang around the most. Rohn would say we could tell the quality of our health, attitude, and income by looking at the people around us. He believed that we start to

> We become the combined average of the five people we hang around the most.

eat what they eat, talk like they talk, read what they read, think like they think, watch what they watch, and dress like they dress.

I like the way Sue Enquist sees the issue. Enquist has been called the John Wooden of women's softball. She played for UCLA from 1975 to 1978, returned in 1980 as an assistant coach, and then served as head coach from 1989 to 2006. As player and coach, she helped win a total of eleven NCAA softball titles. She retired with a career coaching record of 887-175-1—an .835 winning percentage that puts her among the top five NCAA coaches of all time.

Enquist has espoused the 33 Percent Rule. She says you can divide people in school, on your team, at work, or anywhere else into the bottom, middle, and top thirds, and they always have the same characteristics: The bottom third suck the life out of you because nothing is ever good enough for them. They take energy and motivation *out* of an environment. The middle third are happy and positive when things are going well, but down in times of adversity. Circumstances dictate their attitude. The top third maintains a positive attitude even in tough times. They are leaders, influencers, and game-changers. Those are the kind of people we should try to be and those are the kind of people we should spend our time with.

It is not always comfortable, but it is always profitable to associate with people larger than ourselves. As the Italian proverb says, "Keep company with good men and you will increase their number."

What kinds of "larger" people should we spend our time with? People with integrity. People who are positive. People who are ahead of us professionally. People who lift us up instead of knocking us down. People who take the high road, never the low. And above all, people who are growing. They should be like Ralph Waldo Emerson and Henry David Thoreau, whose question for each other whenever they met was, "What have your learned since we last met?"

I highly recommend that you also find an accountability partner to take the growth journey with you. That person will help you to stick with your right decisions and help you avoid making wrong ones. A good accountability partner should:

Love you unconditionally.
Desire your success.
Be mature.
Ask you agreed-upon questions.
Help you when you need help.

You cannot take the growth journey alone, not if you want to reach your potential. The most significant factor in any person's environment is the people.

If you change nothing else in your life for the better than that, you will have increased your chances of success tenfold. So think long and hard about who you're spending the most time with, for wherever they are headed, so are you.

4. Challenge Yourself in Your New Environment

I once heard a story about a Japanese artist who painted a picture on a large canvas. Down in one corner was a tree and on the limbs of the tree were some birds. The rest of the canvas was bare. When he was asked if he was going to paint something more to fill the rest of the canvas, he said, "Oh no, I have to leave room for the birds to fly."

One of the most positive things about being in a growth environment is that it gives you room to fly, but you must be intentional about finding and creating those growth opportunities. You must develop the habit and discipline of challenging yourself.

One of the first ways that I challenged myself was by making my goals public. Few things push a person like a deadline and an audience. That didn't mean that I always reached my goals. But I found that if I told others about what I intended to do, I worked harder, and I worked in such a way that I wouldn't be ashamed of my efforts even if everyone was watching them.

Another way I've challenged myself—both when I started and still today—is to look for one major growth opportunity every week, follow through on it, and learn from it. Whether it's a meeting with friends, a learning lunch with a mentor, a conference I'm attending, or a speaking event where I might get time with high-profile leaders, I always prepare the same way—by asking five questions before the learning time. I ask:

- **What are their strengths?** This is where I'll learn the most.
- **What are they learning now?** This is how I can catch their passion.
- **What do I need right now?** This helps me to apply what I learn to my situation.
- **Who have they met, what have they read, or what have they done that has helped them?** This helps me to find additional growth opportunities.
- **What haven't I asked that I should have?** This enables them to point out changes I need to make from their perspective.

A better growth environment won't help you much if you don't do everything in your power to make the most of it. It's like an entrepreneur being given money for new opportunities and never using it. You must seize the growth opportunities you have and make the most of them by challenging yourself.

5. Focus on the Moment

The changes we want to make in our lives come only in the present. What we do *now* controls who we become and where we are in the future. We live and work in the present. As Harvey Firestone Jr. said, "Today is when everything that's going to happen from now on begins." If you need to make changes in yourself and your environment, don't worry about your past.

> "Today is when everything that's going to happen from now on begins."
> —Harvey Firestone Jr.

I read that former movie star and diplomat Shirley Temple Black learned about the power of living in the moment from her mother-in-law. Evidently when her husband, Charles, was a boy, he asked his mother, "What was the happiest moment of your life?"

"This moment, right now," she responded.

"But what about all the other happy moments in your life? What about when you were married?" he asked.

She laughed and said, "My happiest moment then was then. My happiest moment now is now. You can only really live in the moment you're in. So to me that's always the happiest moment."

Mother Teresa observed, "Yesterday is gone. Tomorrow has not yet come. We have only today. Let us begin." If you need to make changes in yourself and your environment, don't dwell on your past. You can't change it. Don't worry about your future. You can't control it. Focus on the current moment and what you can do now.

6. Move Forward Despite Criticism

In his classic *The Science of Getting Rich,* author Wallace D. Wattles writes, "Do not wait for a change of environment before you act. Cause a change of environment through action. You can act upon your present environment so as to cause yourself to be transferred to a better environment."[2]

Growth always comes from taking action, and taking action almost always brings criticism. Move forward anyway. To reach your potential, you must do not only what others believe you cannot do, but what even *you* believe you cannot do. Most people underestimate themselves. They shoot for what they know they can reach. Instead they should reach for what's beyond their grasp. If you don't try to create the future you want, you must endure the future you get.

As you take action to change yourself and your environment, you will almost certainly be criticized for it. Poet Ralph Waldo Emerson observed, "What-

> "Whatever course you decide upon, there is always someone to tell you that you are wrong."
>
> —*Ralph Waldo Emerson*

ever course you decide upon, there is always someone to tell you that you are wrong. There are always difficulties arising which tempt you to believe that your critics are right. To map out a plan of action and follow it to the end requires some of the same courage which a soldier needs. Peace has its victories, but it takes brave men to win them."

When I was sensing that I needed to change environments in my career, the organization offered me the best position they had. It was a very generous thing for them to do, but I knew with great certainty that I had to make a transition and go in a different direction, so I declined their offer. Unfortunately, they felt rejected. And they criticized my decision. That's okay. As speaker Les Brown says, "Someone's opinion of you does not have to become your reality." Their words hurt, but they didn't make me question my decision.

Albert F. Geoffrey asserts, "When you take charge of your life, there is no longer need to ask permission of other people or society at large. When you ask permission you give someone veto power over your life." Before making a major change, seek wise counsel if you can, but make your own decisions. You are ultimately accountable for the choices you make in your life.

A Note for Leaders

As I grew in my career and began leading larger organizations, my growth challenge began to change. The need for me to grow was always there, and the need to find people who teach me never changed. However, as the leader of an organization, I came to recognize that it was my responsibility to create a positive growth environment for others. I did that by using the same list I created for myself in 1973 and applying it to help others. I strove to create a place where . . .

Others are ahead of them.
They are continually challenged.
Their focus is forward.
The atmosphere is affirming.
They are often out of their comfort zone.
They wake up excited.
Failure is not their enemy.
Others are growing.

People desire change.

Growth is modeled and expected.

As the leader, it was my responsibility to take the initiative and create such an environment. It was hard work, but the effort was always worth it. Many people blossomed, grew, and became leaders as a result.

When leaders match people to roles in the organization, it's not enough for them to weigh what people have done in the past. They must also consider what people could do if the environment allowed them to flourish. Likewise, it's a good idea to help people understand what will be missing for them when they leave a growth environment. I always tried to do that during exit interviews with people as they moved on from any of my organizations. I'd tell them, "You are leaving an environment where growth is a priority and people are encouraged and expected to develop. If you don't go to a similar environment, you can't expect to get the same results. And you'll have to work extra hard to keep growing."

Some understood and met the challenges ahead of them. Others saw only what they hoped would be greener pastures and didn't understand the importance of a good environment until they hit walls they'd never experienced before.

Never forget the Law of Environment: Growth

thrives in conducive surroundings. If you are in a positive growth environment, be grateful. Thank the people who have helped to create it, and reward them by striving to reach your potential. If you're not, do what you must to change your environment and yourself. And if you are a leader, do everything in your power to grow yourself and create the right environment in which others can grow. It will be the best investment you ever made as a leader.

Applying
the Law of Environment
to Your Life

1. Assess your current environment when it comes to growth by answering true or false to each of the following ten statements:
   1. Others are ahead of me.
   2. I am continually challenged.
   3. My focus is forward.
   4. The atmosphere is affirming.
   5. I am often out of my comfort zone.
   6. I wake up excited.
   7. Failure is not my enemy.
   8. Others are growing.
   9. People desire change.
   10. Growth is modeled and expected.

If you answer false to more than five of the statements, your current environment may be hampering your growth. You will need to determine whether you need to change or improve your environment in order to reach your potential.

2. Assess your personal-growth needs in the three main areas mentioned in the chapter:

THE RIGHT SOIL TO GROW IN: WHAT NOURISHES ME? GROWTH.

Use the following list from the chapter or create your own to assess what nurtures you:

Music—What songs lift me?
Thoughts—What ideas speak to me?
Experiences—What experiences rejuvenate me?
Friends—What people encourage me?
Recreation—What activities revive me?
Soul—What spiritual exercises strengthen me?
Hopes—What dreams inspire me?
Home—What family members care for me?
Giftedness—What blessings activate me?
Memories—What recollections make me smile?
Books—What have I read that changed me?

THE RIGHT AIR TO BREATHE IN: WHAT KEEPS ME ALIVE? PURPOSE.

Review your answers to the questions at the end of the Law of Awareness and the Law of Consistency chapters. Use them to develop a purpose statement for your life. Don't expect it to be perfect or permanent. It will probably continue to grow and change as you do, but it will give you a stronger sense of direction now.

THE RIGHT CLIMATE TO LIVE IN: WHAT SUSTAINS ME? PEOPLE.

Make a list of the people who are currently most influential in your life: friends, family, colleagues, employers, mentors, and so on. Be sure to also include anyone you spend a substantial amount of time with. Then scan the list and determine who on the list is "larger" than you: more skilled or more talented, farther ahead professionally, more solid in character or in any other significant way. If the majority of people are not stretching you, you need to find additional people who will help you change and grow.

3. Significant growth will not occur in your life if you are not continually challenged in your environment. Set specific goals for yourself that are beyond your current capabilities. In addition, review your calendar for the upcoming month. Look for the best potential growth opportunity in each week and plan for it by asking yourself questions similar to the ones contained in the chapter.

7

The Law of Design

To Maximize Growth, Develop Strategies

*"If you don't design your own life plan,
chances are you'll fall into someone
else's plan. And guess what they may
have planned for you? Not much."*
—JIM ROHN

What is your favorite time of year? Is it Christmas? Is it when you celebrate your birthday? Or when flowers bloom in the spring? Or your summer vacation? Or when the children go back to school? Or the beginning of football season? Or when the leaves change? When is it? I can tell you mine. It's the week after Christmas.

Glancing Backward—Planning Forward

On Christmas Day in the afternoon, after the grandchildren have finished opening all their presents and all the hoopla has died down, I can hardly contain myself, because I know it's time for one of the things I love most every year. I steal off to my study while everyone else is watching television or napping. There on my desk waiting for me is my appointment calendar from the preceding year and a yellow legal pad. Starting that afternoon and continuing that week up until New Year's Eve, I spend time reviewing my calendar. I review every appointment, meeting, commitment, and activity—hour by hour—from the previous 359 days. And I evaluate each of them.

I look carefully at my speaking engagements and consider what I should do more of, what I should do less of, and what I should eliminate altogether.

I look at the growth opportunities I pursued and judge which gave a high return and which didn't.

I look at all the meetings and appointments I had and determine which ones I should do more of and which I should eliminate.

I consider how much time I spent doing things that I should have delegated to someone else. (I also look at what I delegated and reconsider whether I should pick anything back up or delegate it to someone different.)

I evaluate whether I spent enough time with my family. I also make a list of all the things Margaret and I did together that year, and I take her out to dinner one night so we can reminisce and enjoy them once again. That's a romantic evening that always ends well!

I try to account for every waking hour I had the previous year. And what's the value of that? It helps me to develop strategies for the coming year. Because I do this every year (and have for decades), I become more focused, strategic, and effective *every year*. Even if I have a difficult time or relatively unproductive year compared to what I desired, it's never a loss, because I learn from it and improve upon it in the coming year. There's no substitute for being strategic. To maximize growth, you must develop strategies. That's the Law of Design.

Life Lessons

Most people allow their lives to simply happen to them. They float along. They wait. They react. And by the time a large portion of their life is behind them, they realize they should have been more proactive and strategic. I hope that hasn't been true for you. If it has, then I want to encourage you to develop a stronger sense of urgency and a pro-strategic mindset. As you plan and develop strategies for your life and growth, I want to share with you some of the things I've learned that have helped me in the process.

1. Life Is Very Simple but Keeping It That Way Is Very Difficult

Despite what others might say, I believe life is pretty simple. It's a matter of knowing your values, making some key decisions based on those values, and then managing those decisions on a day-to-day basis. That's pretty straightforward. And at least in theory, the longer we live and the more we learn, the more experience and the more knowledge we acquire that should make life even simpler. But life has a way of *becoming* complicated, and it is only through great effort that we can keep it simple.

A few years ago I attended a conference on Global Strategies for Leaders. While we were there, we were divided into groups for some strategic thinking time. I was fortunate to be placed with Neil Cole. Although I did not know him prior to that day, I became impressed very quickly during our discussion time by his ability to design simple, effective strategies.

During a break I asked Neil for advice for designing a strategy to develop leaders globally. He replied,

"The secret is found in simplicity." He then shared with me the following three questions that he said would be key to making such a strategy work:

- **Can it be received personally?** A profound implication—it must be internalized and transform the soul of the leader.
- **Can it be repeated easily?** Simple application—it must be passed on after only a brief encounter.
- **Can it be transferred strategically?** A universal communication—it must be passed on globally to all cultural contexts.

My encounter with Neil made a strong impression on me. I later used those questions at EQUIP as we developed our Million Leader Mandate strategy to train one million leaders worldwide. I also came away from that conversation with a determination to design my life as simply as possible by discovering and developing systems for my success. Those systems help me fight the battle against complexity in my life every day. I believe they can help you too. Just remember as you develop strategies for growth to keep them personal, repeatable, and transferrable. A beautifully conceived strategy does you no good if you can't use it.

2. Designing Your Life Is More Important Than Designing Your Career

Oscar-winning actress Reese Witherspoon says, "Many people worry so much about managing their careers but rarely spend half that much energy managing their lives. I want to make my life, not just my job, the best it can be. The rest will work itself out."

I think Witherspoon's advice is partially correct: If you plan your life well, then your career will work itself out. The problem is that most people don't spend very much time planning their careers either. They spend more time planning for Christmas or their vacation. Why? Because people focus on what they think will give them the greatest return. If you don't believe you can succeed in your life in the long term, you're not very likely to give it the planning attention it deserves.

Planning your life is about finding yourself, knowing who you are, and then customizing a design for your growth. Once you draw the blueprint for your life, then you can apply it to your career.

3. Life Is Not a Dress Rehearsal!

As you may have guessed by now, I'm a longtime reader of Charles Schulz's comic strip *Peanuts*. Schulz captured the feelings of many people in a strip in which Charlie Brown says to Linus, "Life is just too much for me. I've been confused from the day I was born. I think the whole trouble is that we're thrown into life too fast. We're not really prepared."

Linus responds, "What did you want...a chance to warm up first?"

There is no warm-up for life, no dress rehearsal, yet that's the way many people seem to be treating it. Each of us goes on stage cold, with no preparation, and we have to figure it out as we go along. That can be messy. We fail. We make mistakes. But we still need to give it our best from the very start.

Regret over not being proactive enough is a common theme among people looking back on their lives. In his book *Aspire*, Kevin Hall tells about a trip he made with a group of Boy Scouts and his desire to inspire them to set bold goals for themselves. He did that by telling them about a study of retired successful executives conducted by Gerald Bell, a noted behavioral scientist. Hall writes,

> I told them what those seventy-year-old executives answered when Dr. Bell asked them what they would do differently if they could live their lives over again.
>
> Their response, an answer that ranked far ahead of any others, was this: *I should have*

taken charge of my life and set my goals earlier. Life isn't practice, it's the real thing.

I shared the rest of the survey answers with the Scouts: *2) I would have taken better care of my health. 3) I would have managed my money better. 4) I would have spent more time with my family. 5) I would have spent more time on personal development. 6) I would have had more fun. 7) I would have planned my career better. 8) I would have given more back.*[1] [emphasis in original]

We don't get a rehearsal for life. We have to do the best we can in the moment. But we can learn from others who have gone before us, people like the executives that Bell studied. They should inspire us to plan as best we can and then give our all. Comedian Fred Allen once said, "You only live once. But if you work it right, once is enough."

> "You only live once. But if you work it right, once is enough."
> —*Fred Allen*

4. In Planning Your Life, Multiply Everything by Two

My outlook on life is primarily optimistic and as a result, my expectations for myself and others tend to be rather unrealistic. Over the course of time, I've learned that the important things in life usually take longer than we expect and cost more than we anticipate. That is especially true when it comes to personal growth. So what do I do to compensate? I multiply by two. If I think something will take me an hour to do, I plan for double to stay out of trouble. If I think a project will take a week to accomplish, I allot two. If I think a goal will require $1,000 to fund, I set aside $2,000. Two isn't a magic number—it just seems to work for me. I've found that multiplying everything by two infuses realism into my optimism.

I'm aware that I'm an especially impatient person, but I think all people naturally desire for things to come to them quickly and easily, including personal growth. The secret isn't really to want more or want it faster. It's to put more time and attention into what you have and what you can do now. Give three times the effort and energy to growing yourself. And allow yourself to grow slowly and with deep roots. Remember that a squash vine or tomato plant grows in a matter of weeks, produces for several days or weeks, and then dies when the first frost comes. In comparison, a tree grows slowly—over years, decades, or even centuries; it produces fruit for decades; and if healthy, it stands up to frost, storms, and drought.

As you develop strategies for growth, give yourself

the time and resources you need. Whatever amounts seem reasonable to you, multiply them by two. That practice will help to keep you from becoming discouraged and giving up too soon.

To Develop Strategies, Depend on Systems

Most accomplishments in life come more easily if you approach them strategically. Rarely does a haphazard approach to anything succeed. And even the few times a nonstrategic approach to achievement comes to fruition, it's not repeatable. So how do you accomplish something strategically on a consistent basis? By creating and using systems. One of the greatest secrets to my personal growth and high productivity is that I use systems for everything.

I have a system for growing personally and gleaning information. I try to read four books every month. I pick two that I can go through fairly quickly and two that I want to really dig into. I also listen to CDs in my car. When I was preaching a weekly sermon as a pastor, I used to listen to five every week. I'd give a CD five minutes. If it was bad, I'd stop listening. If it was good, I'd listen to the whole thing. If it was great, I'd stop listening after five minutes and set the CD aside to have it transcribed so I could read every word.

I have a system for capturing and filing all the good stories, quotes, and articles that I read. If I find an article I like, I rip it out of the magazine or journal, write at the top the topic it should be filed under, and set it aside for my assistant to put into my files. As I read a book, when I find a quote or story I like, I mark the page, write the topic I want it filed under, and write the page number where it can be found on the inside front cover of the book. When I'm done reading the book, I give it to my assistant, and she photocopies the quotes or types them up, and puts them in my quotes files.

This practice has changed my life. Most people I know who take the time to grow personally don't take the time to capture the best thoughts and ideas they come across. They spend hours or days looking for a story they once read or a quote they can't quite recall. *Didn't I read something about that recently?* they wonder. *Now, which book was that in?* Maybe they are able to find it. Maybe not. Do you know how much time it takes me to find something I read and want to recall? Two minutes or less. Usually I can walk over to my desk and put my hand on it in under a minute. If I can't recall what topic I filed it under and have to check two or three topics, it might take me as long as five minutes.

I have a system for thinking. I keep about a dozen

quotes or ideas in the Notes app on my iPhone, which I have with me all the time. I refer to them throughout the day so they can really sink into my mind and heart. When I swim laps every day, I choose one or two thoughts (or sometimes a couple of prayer items) to roll over in my mind while I swim. And I also have my thinking chair. If I wake up in the middle of the night, which is a fairly common occurrence, I slip down into my office with a legal pad to think and write.

I have a system for writing. Before I take a major trip, which can last up to two or three weeks, I spend a day or longer preparing what I need to write. If I'm working on a book, I create a notebook with raw material. If the outline for the book has fifteen chapters (as this one does), I put together a binder with fifteen numbered tabs. If I already have some thoughts about a particular chapter, I three-hole punch it and put it behind that tab. I also go into my quote and article files and photocopy any material that I think I might want to use for that chapter. I three-hole punch those pages and put them behind that tab. If I've written a lesson on that subject, I copy it, three-hole punch it, and put it behind the tab. By the time I'm done, I've got an entire binder of material hand-picked for every chapter. With that, a legal pad, tape, and a pen, I'm ready to write whether I'm on a plane, in a hotel room, or staying at a relative's house.

I have a system for planning my days. I look at my calendar six weeks out so I know what's coming and can plan my work. And every morning, I review my schedule for the day and ask myself, *What is the main event?* I make sure I know the most important thing that I must win that day, no matter what else happens.

I even have systems for waiting in lines and other mundane activities. For example, if I'm at a ballgame with friends and we go to the concession stand to get food, if there are three lines, I stand in one and ask friends to stand in the other two. When one of us gets to the counter first, then we all go to that person and place our orders together. That way we save time.

Strategies and systems are a way of life for me. Michael Gerber, author of *The E-Myth*, says that "systems permit ordinary people to achieve extraordinary results predictably. However, without a system, even extraordinary people find it difficult to predictably achieve even ordinary results." I totally agree with that.

> "Systems permit ordinary people to achieve extraordinary results predictably."
> —*Michael Gerber*

What is a system? It's a process for predictably achieving a goal based on specific, orderly, repeatable principles and practices. Systems leverage your time, money, and abilities. They are great tools for personal growth. Systems are deliberate, intentional, and practical. They really work—regardless of your profession, talent level, or experience. They improve your performance. A life without any systems is a life where the person must face every task and challenge from scratch.

What Systems Include

If you want to make the most of your personal growth by getting the most you can out of every effort and doing it as efficiently as possible, you need to develop systems that work for you. That will be a personal thing, because your systems need to be tailored to you. However, as you strive to create them, keep the following guidelines in mind:

1. Effective Systems Take the Big Picture into Account

Stephen Covey observed, "We may be very busy, we may be very efficient, but we will also be truly effective only when we begin with the end in mind." When I started creating systems for my personal growth, they were very targeted. I knew I would be speaking every week of my life. I knew I would be leading people and organizations. As I approached age thirty, I realized that I wanted to write books.

My efforts had to support and advance my abilities in those areas.

People who excel, regardless of their profession, develop systems to help them achieve the big picture. A good example of that was Muhammad Ali's preparation for the "Rumble in the Jungle" fight against George Foreman on October 30, 1974. It's true that Ali was a great athlete—THE greatest, according to him. But physically he was no match for Foreman, who was a powerful puncher. Virtually nobody thought Ali had a chance.

Joe Frazier and Ken Norton had beaten Ali previously, and George Foreman had knocked out both of those fighters in the second round. But Ali could see Foreman's weakness—his lack of staying power—and Ali figured out a system that would allow him to overcome the stronger boxer. Ali called it the "Rope-a-Dope." Ali would lean back against the ropes, shielding himself while Foreman pounded away, trying to knock him out. For seven rounds, Foreman threw hundreds of punches, and Ali let the storm blow over him. By round eight, Ali could see that Foreman had worn himself out. That's when Ali dropped Foreman with a combination and reclaimed the heavyweight championship of the world.

It's not enough to be busy. If you're busy planning, busy reading books, and busy going to conferences, but they aren't targeted on the areas essential to your success, you're not helping yourself. As the saying goes, unhappiness is not knowing what we want and killing ourselves to get it.

> Unhappiness is not knowing what we want and killing ourselves to get it.

What is your big picture? In what areas must you grow to achieve your purpose? Author and professor C. S. Lewis said, "Every person is composed of a few themes." What are yours? And what systems can you develop to advance yourself in those areas today and every day? I had to stop reading books simply for pleasure and read books that would help me in my areas of strength. I also took two speed-reading classes to help me improve. What must you do?

> "Every person is composed of a few themes."
> —C. S. Lewis

2. Effective Systems Make Use of Priorities

A system is of limited help to you if it doesn't take into account your priorities. Brian Tracy says, "Perhaps the very best question you can memorize and repeat over and over is, 'What is the most valuable use of my time right now?'" Your answer to that question should shape any system you create for yourself. You should also ask yourself, "*When* is my most valuable time?" because you'll want to always make the most of it. For me it's mornings. When I recognized that, I stopped scheduling any breakfast meetings. That was thirty years ago. Imagine how much of my prime time would have gotten used up if I'd allowed myself to meet with people, which I'm capable of doing *anytime,* during my prime productivity time.

Making that decision for me was pretty easy. Others have been more difficult. I am very opportunity driven, and I tend to want to do everything. If one is good, four is better. I love saying yes. I have a very hard time saying no. As a result, I get spread too thin. To deal with that, I had to develop a system. I was no longer allowed to answer requests for my time. Instead, requests had to go to a group who would decide whether or not I would accept a speaking engagement or other request. We fondly named them the Hatchet Committee. Why? Because they put the ax to ninety percent of the requests that came in. It was the only system that I could find that forced me to maintain my priorities when it came to my time.

What systems do you need to put into place to help you maintain your priorities? And what people do you need to give responsibility and power to so they can help you?

3. Effective Systems Include Measurement

Jack Welch, former CEO of General Electric, asserted, "Strategy is first trying to understand where you sit in today's world. Not where you wish you were or where you hoped you would be, but where you are. Then it's trying to understand where you want to be five years out. Finally, it's assessing the realistic chances of getting from here to there." What do all three of these actions—knowing where you are, where you want to be, and the chances of getting there—have in common? Measurement. Any kind of progress requires the ability to measure, and for that reason, your systems must include a way to measure your results.

When I first moved to Atlanta from San Diego, I was surprised by how congested and difficult traffic was in the area. Road building seemed to run about ten years behind population growth. I couldn't do anything about the roads, but I was determined to improve my ability to get around. What was my solution? For the first six months I explored alternate routes to my most common destinations, and I tracked the mileage and time it took on every route. I discovered five different routes to the Atlanta airport, and I knew which one to take based on the time of day and the different traffic scenarios. I could have been a limo driver!

H. James Harrington, former engineer, IBM executive, and performance improvement pioneer, says, "Measurement is the first step that leads to control and eventually to improvement. If you can't measure something, you can't understand it. If you can't understand it, you can't control it. If you can't control it, you can't improve it."

Think about it: Where would businesspeople be if they had no way of measuring their profits? Where would sales and marketing people be if they had no idea how many leads turned into sales or how many people responded to advertising? Where would sports teams be if they never knew the score of the game? Measurement is key to improvement. In fact, measurement itself can even create improvement. Researchers who conducted experiments in productivity at the Hawthorne Works Plant outside Chicago in the 1930s discovered that when people knew their work was being measured, their productivity increased. Researchers called that the Hawthorne Effect.

> When people know their work is being measured, their productivity increases.

Measurement makes a difference. It enables you to

set goals, evaluate progress, judge results, and diagnose problems. If you want to stimulate your growth progress and evaluate the results, build measurement into your systems.

4. Effective Systems Include Application

If you had the most beautiful blueprints in the world for the most spectacular home, what value would they have if there was no action plan to build it? Not much. That's why William Danforth, the founder of Nestlé Purina, said, "No plan is worth the paper it is printed on unless it starts you doing something."

I've been a fan of Ohio State University football for decades, and for several years while Jim Tressel was head coach of the team, I had the privilege of speaking to the team before their annual game with Michigan and then watching the game on the sidelines. What a wonderful experience. Once while I was there I noticed a sign that asked players and coaches one simple question: "What are you going to do now?"

That's a great question for us to ask ourselves every time we go out onto our "playing field." What are we going to *do*? It's not enough just to plan, though planning is important. Both plan and action must go together. The plan creates the track. The action provides the traction. So anytime you have a goal but you think you won't be able to reach it, don't adjust the goal. Adjust the action steps.

People who develop systems that include action steps are almost always more successful than people who don't. Even less talented people with fewer resources accomplish more if they have developed the habit of taking action. That's one of the reasons I've developed the habit of asking myself three questions every time I learn something new:

- Where can I use this?
- When can I use this?
- Who needs to know this?

This has become a discipline in my life, so I always have a bias toward action when I learn something new.

5. Effective Systems Employ Organization

I once saw a sign in a cluttered country store that read, "We've got it, if you can find it." That's not much of a help, is it? I mentioned earlier in the chapter that I have a system for filing quotes. Why did I develop that? Because the number one time waster for most people is looking for things that are lost.

> The number one time waster for most people is looking for things that are lost.

My choleric personality and the heavy workload of my career prompted me to start developing systems. In the beginning it was the only way I could be sure to get things done. And even though as my career developed I was able to hire an assistant and then additional staff members, I continued to use systems to keep myself and my interaction with staff and co-workers organized. For example, I touch base with my assistant, Linda Eggers, at least once a day, every day—365 days a year. It doesn't matter if I'm home in Florida or on the road in China.

I also have a way of organizing my calendar—or more accurately, asking Linda to organize my calendar. Family activities go on the calendar first. Why? Because they are my highest priority. Everything else has to fit around them.

Time has a way of getting away from most people, yet time is what life is made of. Everything we do requires time, yet many people take it for granted. How you spend your time is more important than how you spend your money. Money mistakes can be corrected. But once time has passed, it's gone forever.

Being organized gives a sense of power. When you know your purpose and priorities and you have

> Being organized gives a sense of power.

ordered your day, week, or year according to them, you have a clarity of thought that strengthens everything you do. You develop an efficiency that helps you to follow through on everything you do. There are few things like it. Make sure your systems make you as organized as you can possibly be.

6. Effective Systems Promote Consistency

Journalist Sydney J. Harris observed, "An idealist believes the short run doesn't count. A cynic believes the long run doesn't matter. A realist believes that what is done or left undone in the short run determines the long run." In other words, if you want to succeed in the long run, you must learn to be consistent day in and day out, week in and week out, year in and year out.

You will never change your life until you change something you do daily. The secret of your success is found in your daily routine. So any system you develop needs to promote consistency, and you must follow it consistently.

> The secret of your success is found in your daily routine.

What does it take to develop consistency? A system and the discipline to follow through. I came across the story of an older gentleman at the funeral of fiery NBA basketball coach Bill Musselman in 2000 who approached Bill's son Eric to tell him a story. The gentleman said he was driving down a two-lane highway on the way to Orville, Ohio, when he saw a boy about eleven years old dribbling a basketball with his right hand along the side of the road. The man said he pulled over and asked the boy, "Where are you going?"

Without stopping dribbling, the boy replied, "Orville."

"Do you know Orville is ten miles away?" he asked.

"Yes."

"What are you going to do when you get there?"

"Dribble back home with my left hand."

The old man looked at Eric and said, "That boy was your father." Now that's what I call creating a system and having the discipline to follow through on it!

Despite the dramatic nature of that story of Musselman's efforts to grow as a basketball player, most efforts at consistency are not so exciting. Every now and then, I get requests from people who say they want to spend the day with me. I think they would be very disappointed by how boring my average day is. I'm up early and spend hours at my desk. In the afternoon I exercise and take care of people-related responsibilities. And I usually go to bed by 10:00. It's not exciting, but it is consistent. And it's a system that works for me.

One Golfer's Strategy

I've enjoyed the game of golf for more than forty years. A few years ago, I came across *Harvey Penick's Little Red Book: Lessons and Teachings from a Lifetime in Golf.* It contains tips and anecdotes on golf from a head pro who was a golfer and teacher for more than eighty years.

The author is Harvey Penick, who fell in love with golf as a boy. He started working as a caddy when he was eight years old, and worked his way up at the Austin Country Club in Austin, Texas. When he was a senior in high school, an influential member of the club offered to get him an appointment to West Point. "No thank you, sir," was Harvey's reply. "The only thing in life I want to be is a golf pro."[2] Harvey was running the club as the head pro before he reached the age of twenty.

Harvey's great love was teaching golf. He taught thousands of golfers during his career at the club, which he oversaw as the head pro for fifty years. He also worked as the coach of the golf team at the University of Texas for more than thirty years. Among the pros he taught were Tom Kite, Ben Crenshaw, Mickey Wright, Betsy Rawls, and Kathy Whitworth.

Harvey wanted to become the best he could at teaching golf, and to do that he was very systematic. He treated every student as an individual, whether the person was a first-time golfer, someone with a high handicap who wanted to improve his score, or a tour professional fine-tuning his game. He never allowed one player to watch him give a lesson to another. He was concerned that observers might try to adopt the coaching to their own games when the advice didn't apply to them. And every time Harvey accepted a new player onto his University of Texas team, he would ask about the teaching methods the student's club pro had used. His strategy was always to keep improving as a teacher. Harvey's son, Tinsley, who became a golf pro in his own right, said, "My dad always said that the day he stopped learning would be the day he stopped teaching. He must have been learning right up to the day he died, because he never stopped teaching."[3]

The strategy that made Harvey Penick world famous was his practice of recording observations and practices in a small, red Scribbletex notebook. He began doing it sometime in his twenties. He wanted to record what worked so he could teach it. He did that for more than sixty years. He kept the book locked in his briefcase, and the only person he ever let read it was Tinsley. Harvey's intention was to pass on what he called his Little Red Book to his son when he retired.[4]

Instead, Harvey decided he wanted to share his lifetime of wisdom with others. He partnered with Bud Shrake, a sports writer, to publish the book. It became an instant bestseller and has since become the bestselling sports book of all time. Harvey remarked,

> What made my Little Red Book special was not that what was written in it had never been said before. It was that what it says about golf has stood the test of time.... Whether it is for beginners, medium players, experts or children, anything I say in my book has been tried and tested with success.[5]

As you seek to develop strategies to maximize your growth, you should also seek out principles that have stood the test of time. And like Harvey, don't try to simply adopt someone else's practices as your own. Customize them to yourself. Use them to build your strengths and reach your goals. And remember that, as Jim Rohn said, "If you go to

> "If you go to work on your goals, your goals will go to work on you. If you go to work on your plan, your plan will go to work on you. Whatever good things we build end up building us."
>
> —Jim Rohn

work on your goals, your goals will go to work on you. If you go to work on your plan, your plan will go to work on you. Whatever good things we build end up building us." That is the power of the Law of Design.

Applying
the Law of Design
to Your Life

1. Take some time to assess which areas in your life receive the most of your strategic planning time. Here is a list of areas to get you thinking. Add others that apply to you:

Career
Faith
Family
Health
Hobby
Marriage
Personal Growth
Vacation

Have you been strategic in your approach to designing strategies and systems for your life? If not, why not? If so, where have you placed the most emphasis? Does your past behavior line up with what you *say* your priorities are? How would you like them to be?

2. Begin developing (or refining) systems for yourself that will maximize your time and increase your efficiency. Brainstorm a list of areas where you desire to improve, are experiencing a problem, or sensing an opportunity. Try to create a system to help you for each. As you design them, make sure that each takes into account the following:

The Big Picture—Will the system help you reach your big-picture goals?

Your Priorities—Is the system consistent with your values and commitments?

Measurement—Does the system give you a tangible way to judge if you've succeeded?

Application—Does the system have a built-in bias toward action?

Organization—Does the system make better use of your time than what you're doing now?

Consistency—Can and will you easily repeat the system on a regular basis?

Don't be reluctant to make adjustments to systems you develop or even abandon them if they don't serve you well. However, you may want to try out any system you develop for at least three weeks (the normal time needed to start developing a positive habit) before evaluating its validity.

3. Many people who try to develop strategies for their life and growth make them too complicated. Any system you develop should be simple and straightforward. To test the ones you develop, try this: Explain them to a friend to see if they pass two tests. The first is whether you can explain it clearly. If you can't, it may be too complicated. The second is to see if your friend knows of a better or simpler way of achieving the same goal.

8

The Law of Pain

Good Management of Bad Experiences
Leads to Great Growth

"Every problem introduces a person to himself."
—JOHN MCDONNELL

How do you usually respond to bad experiences? Do you explode in anger? Do you shrink into yourself emotionally? Do you detach yourself from the experience as much as possible? Do you ignore it?

John McDonnell once said, "Every problem introduces a person to himself." What an insight! Each time we encounter a painful experience, we get to know ourselves a little better. Pain can stop us dead in our tracks. Or it can cause us to make decisions we would like to put off, deal with issues we would rather not face, and make changes that make us feel uncomfortable. Pain prompts us to face who we are and where we are. What we do with that experience defines who we become.

Pain Unimaginable

Recently I came across the story of Cheryl McGuinness, someone who lived through about as bad an experience as a person can. One morning in late summer, her husband, Tom, went off to work before dawn, as he often did, kissing her before he left. A few hours later, Cheryl got up, took her teenage daughter and son to school, and settled into her daily routine.

Then she got a phone call from a friend asking if Tom was home. Then another. She knew something was up, but she had no clue what it was. When she pressed for an answer, the friend finally responded, "A plane has been hijacked."

It was the morning of September 11, 2001, and Cheryl's husband, Tom, was a pilot for American Airlines.

For hours, while Cheryl's house filled with friends, neighbors, other pilots, and people from her church, she was unable to get any answers to her questions. But when a car pulled up to her house carrying the chief pilot of the airline, she learned what happened.

American Airlines Flight 11, for which Tom had been the copilot, was the first plane that crashed into the World Trade Center. Tom and all the others on the plane were dead.

Like most people who survive a terrible tragedy, Cheryl coped as best she could. Some individuals manage negative experiences well, while others struggle. According to experts, in the wake of the World Trade Center attacks, many people suffered from severe stress, post-traumatic stress disorder (PTSD), depression, general anxiety disorder (GAD), and substance abuse disorders.[1]

Despite having such a personally tragic connection to the 9/11 attacks, Cheryl did well under the circumstances. In *Beauty Beyond the Ashes*, a book she published three years after the event, she wrote, "As unfair, unreasonable, and impossible as it seems, we still have work to do after a tragedy occurs. We still have roles to fill. We still have responsibilities to family and others. The stuff of life may pause for a while, but it doesn't stop. Fair or not, that is reality."[2]

Cheryl fulfilled her role with determination and strength. She planned Tom's funeral and even spoke at it, which was something far out of her comfort zone. She took care of her children. She started running her household as a single parent. And she learned rapidly how to deal with the difficulties of being a widow. For example, for the first Mother's Day she spent alone after the tragedy, she allowed well-meaning friends to talk her into going to an event that they thought would help her. It was a mistake. So as Father's Day approached, she was proactive and arranged the day to make the best of it for herself and her children.

Each new experience became an opportunity for personal growth. Cheryl writes, "I am learning more each day. The circumstances of 9/11 have forced me to examine who I am, to face myself in ways that I never had to before, to ask, 'What does God want for me? What can I do in him, by his power within me? How will he use me to touch others?' I am learning more about myself and about God. And I am learning it on my own, not through Tom's filter."[3] Cheryl says that she didn't realize until Tom was gone how lazy she had become. Before, she had depended on him to prompt her growth. Now she was taking responsibility for it herself.

One of the areas where she grew the most was in public speaking. "Before 9/11, I had never been a public speaker. The very thought of speaking before a large group frightened me. When I spoke at Tom's memorial service, I put aside my fear for that one day, figuring I'd been given a once-in-a-lifetime opportunity.... I didn't expect to speak in public ever again."[4] But people kept asking her to speak, and step by step, she grew as a speaker. She was determined to allow her loss to lead to others' gain.

Today Cheryl's children are grown. She remarried; her husband is Doug Hutchins. And she is content with her life. She was asked about the tragedy on its tenth anniversary. "It's a terrible, terrible day that I don't think anybody can ever forget," she said, but added, "Out of the ashes of Sept. 11, out of the rubble that day, I can emerge to say that I am stronger today than 10 years ago."[5] That's what can happen when a person manages bad experiences well. That shows the power of the Law of Pain.

What I Know about Bad Experiences

What separates people who thrive from those who merely survive? I believe it's how they face their problems. That's the reason I wrote *Failing Forward*; I wanted to help people to deal with problems and mistakes in a way that helped them rather than hurt them. I wanted to teach people how to use bad experiences as stepping stones for success. I've never known anyone who said, "I love problems," but I've known many who have

> I've never known anyone who said, "I love problems," but I've known many who have admitted that their greatest gains came in the middle of their pain.

admitted that their greatest gains came in the middle of their pain.

Here's what I know about bad experiences:

1. Everyone Has Them

Life is filled with ups and downs. The problem is that what most of us want is ups and ups. That's not possible. I think it's pretty obvious that nobody gets to escape bad experiences. Perhaps that's one of the reasons my speech "How to Do Good When Things Are So Bad" has been so popular. As the saying goes: Some days you're the pigeon; some days you're the statue!

We can do everything in our power to avoid negative experiences, but they have a way of finding us. I love the quote "I try to take life one day at a time, but lately several days have attacked me at once." No matter who you are, where you live, what you do, or what your background is, you will have to deal with bad experiences. As television host and author Dennis Wholey observed, "Expecting the world to treat you fairly just because you're a good person is a little like expecting the bull not to charge you because you're a vegetarian."

> "Expecting the world to treat you fairly just because you're a good person is a little like expecting the bull not to charge you because you're a vegetarian."
> —*Dennis Wholey*

You have to have realistic expectations when it comes to pain and problems. You can't avoid them.

2. No One Likes Them

Academy Award–winning actor Dustin Hoffman described what it was like for him and some fellow actors in the early days of their careers when they were struggling:

> If anyone had told us that we would have been successful, we would have laughed in their face. We were anything but successful actors in those days. I was a waiter, Gene Hackman was a mover and Robert Duvall worked at the post office. We didn't dream of being rich and famous; we dreamed of finding a job. It was a time of terrible rejection, and we hated being rejected. It got to the point that we used to leave our 8x10's at the door of casting agents, knock and run, just so we wouldn't have to be rejected face-to-face again. It was so discouraging that I seriously considered quitting and becoming an acting teacher at a university.

No one likes it when they're in the middle of a bad experience. It's usually just painful. But if they manage the experience well, then they enjoy talking about it afterward. It becomes a great war story.

3. Few People Make Bad Experiences Positive Experiences

Life's difficulties do not allow us to stay the same. They move us. The question is, in which direction will we be moved: forward or backward? When we have bad experiences, do we become better or bitter? Will those experiences limit us or lead us to grow? As Warren G. Lester remarked, "Success in life comes not from holding a good hand, but in playing a poor hand well."

> "Success in life comes not from holding a good hand, but in playing a poor hand well."
>
> —*Warren G. Lester*

When tough times come, many people don't respond well. Some seem to have the motto that I once saw on a bumper sticker: "When the going gets tough, it's time to take a nap." What a shame. Learning the Law of Pain is essential for anyone who wants to grow. Most successful people will point to the hard times in their lives as key points in their journey of development. If you are dedicated to growth, then you must become committed to managing your bad experiences well.

My Pain File

Everyone has a pain file. You've got yours; I've got mine. I may not have experienced anything as traumatic as Cheryl McGuinness did, but I've had my share of failures and negative experiences. Here are a few that have become gains in growth over the long run:

- **The Pain of Inexperience**—I expected instant success early in my career but stumbled often because of my immaturity. I had to learn patience and earn respect and influence from others.
- **The Pain of Incompetence**—I did a lot of counseling early in my career and was terrible at it. That forced me to reevaluate my gifting. Only when I started equipping people did I find my strength zone.
- **The Pain of Disappointment**—Margaret and I were scheduled to adopt a son but then "lost" him. We were devastated. Six months later we adopted our son, Joel, who is a great joy to our lives.
- **The Pain of Conflict**—One church I led experienced a split in the congregation, and some people left the church. That experience made me dig deeper as a leader.

- **The Pain of Change**—I've already told you about how early in my career I changed organizations. That meant I had to start over. Though difficult, it afforded me many opportunities.
- **The Pain of Bad Health**—My heart attack at age fifty-one was excruciating. It was also an eye-opener. I immediately changed my eating habits and bought into the practice of daily exercise.
- **The Pain of Hard Decisions**—Wanting everyone to be happy and making tough decisions were incompatible tasks. I learned that good leadership is disappointing people at a rate they can stand.
- **The Pain of Financial Loss**—A bad investment decision cost us greatly. It wasn't fun selling my assets to cover it. It helped me to be more careful in risk taking.
- **The Pain of Relationship Losses**—Striving to reach my potential has separated me from friends who had no desire to grow. As I developed new friendships, I learned to build relationships with growing people who wanted to take the journey with me.
- **The Pain of Not Being Number One**—In one job I followed a wonderful founding pastor who was greatly loved as a leader. For some people, I

was never as loved or respected as much he was. That taught me humility.

- **The Pain of Traveling**—My career has kept me on the road. It taught me to value my family and motivated me to make the most of our time together.

- **The Pain of Responsibility**—Leading organizations and having many people depend on me has required me to think of others' well-being, continually create new content, keep my calendar full, and constantly meet demanding deadlines. This has been very tiring. But it also has taught me a lot about priorities and self-discipline.

> Wanting everyone to be happy and making tough decisions were incompatible tasks. I learned that good leadership is disappointing people at a rate they can stand.

What have all these painful experiences taught me? To let my discomfort be a catalyst for my development. Growth is the best possible outcome for any negative experience.

How to Turn Your Pain into Gain

Frank Hughes quipped, "Experience isn't really the best teacher but it sure does serve as the best excuse for not trying to do the same silly thing again." If you want your bad experiences to keep you not only from doing the same silly things but to also lead to significant growth, I suggest that you embrace the following five actions:

> "Experience isn't really the best teacher but it sure does serve as the best excuse for not trying to do the same silly thing again."
> —Frank Hughes

1. Choose a Positive Life Stance

"Life stance" is a term used to describe people's overall frame of reference—the set of attitudes, assumptions, and expectations people hold about themselves, other people, and the world in general. It comprises, for instance, people's attitudes toward money, assumptions about their health, and expectations for their children's future. The product of any person's life stance is their overall way of looking at things: whether they tend to be optimistic or pessimistic, cheerful or gloomy, trusting or suspicious, friendly or reserved, brave or timid, generous or stingy, giving or selfish. If you can maintain a positive life stance, you put yourself in the best position to manage bad experiences and turn them into positive growth.

Family therapy pioneer and author Virginia Satir observed, "Life is not the way it's supposed to be. It's

> "Life is not the way it's supposed to be. It's the way it is. The way you cope with it is what makes the difference."
>
> —Virginia Satir

the way it is. The way you cope with it is what makes the difference." You cannot control much of what happens to you in life. However, you can control your attitude. And you can choose to rise above your circumstances and refuse to allow negative experiences to undermine who you are and what you believe. And you can be resolved to find something positive to learn in the face of tragedy, as Cheryl McGuinness did.

I have come to adopt a positive life stance because I believe it gives me the best chance to succeed while putting me in the best position to help others succeed. I came to develop this mind-set by way of the following thinking:

- Life is filled with good and bad.
- Some of the good and bad I can't control—that's life.
- Some of the good and bad will find me.
- If I have a positive life stance the good and bad will become better.
- If I have a negative life stance the good and bad will become worse.
- Therefore I choose a positive life stance.

To a large degree in life, you get what you expect—not always, but most of the time. So why would I want to expect the worst? Instead, I try to follow the idea expressed by poet John Greenleaf Whittier when he wrote,

No longer forward nor behind
I look in hope or fear;
But, grateful, take the good I find,
The best of now and here.

If you can do that, you not only make the life you have more livable, you also make life's lessons more learnable.

2. Embrace and Develop Your Creativity

There's a story about a chicken farmer whose land was flooded nearly every spring. He didn't want to give up his farm and move, but when the water backed up onto his land and flooded his chicken coops, it was always a struggle to get his chickens to higher ground. Some years he couldn't move fast enough and hundreds of his chickens drowned.

After the worst spring he'd ever experienced and losing his entire flock, he came into the farmhouse and told his wife, "I've had it. I can't afford to buy another place. I can't sell this one. I don't know what to do."

His wife replied, "Buy ducks."

The people who make the most of bad experiences are the ones who find creative ways to meet them, like the farmer's wife in the story. They see possibilities within their problems.

Author Neale Donald Walsh asserted, "Life begins at the end of your comfort zone." I believe that cre-

> "Life begins at the end of your comfort zone."
>
> —Neale Donald Walsh

ativity begins at the end of your comfort zone. When you feel the pain of bad experiences, creativity gives you the opportunity to turn that pain into gain. The secret to doing that is to use the energy that comes from either adrenaline or anger and use it to solve problems and learn lessons.

I experienced this many years ago when I was invited by Lloyd Ogilvie to contribute to *The Communicator's Commentary*, a series of twenty-one books of biblical commentary on the Old Testament. Lloyd asked me to write the commentary on the book of Deuteronomy, and I agreed. But it didn't take me long to realize I was in way over my head. I'm no Old Testament scholar. Trying to write that book was a terrible experience. Three different times I went to Lloyd asking to be released from the agreement, and all three times he declined, encouraging me to keep working at it.

The bad news was that I was failing at the task and I was miserable about it. The good news is that because he wouldn't take no for an answer, I had to become creative. I started to interview biblical scholars to gain their perspective. And because my Hebrew wasn't strong enough, I hired Professor William Yarchin to tutor me in Hebrew. Those actions, plus a lot of hard work, enabled me to finish the task. And when all of the volumes in the series were published, I asked the other twenty authors to sign copies of theirs. Today that collection sits on the shelf of my library as a treasured possession!

When you have a bad experience, instead of letting it discourage you or make you angry, try to find a way to let it prompt your creativity.

3. Embrace the Value of Bad Experiences

President John F. Kennedy was once asked how he became a war hero. With his customary dry wit he responded, "It was quite easy. Somebody sunk my boat." It's always easier to see something positive in a negative experience *long after* it happens. It's difficult to meet the negative experience in the moment with a positive mind-set. However, if you can do that, you will always be able to learn something from it.

Inventor Charles F. Kettering, who was the head of research at General Motors, said, "You will never stub your toe standing still. The faster you go, the more chance there is of stubbing your toe, but the more chance you have of getting somewhere." In other words, where there is no struggle, there is no progress. Facing difficulties is inevitable. Learning from them is optional. Whether you learn is based on if you understand that difficulties present opportunities to learn and treat them accordingly.

> Facing difficulties is inevitable. Learning from them is optional.

4. Make Good Changes after Learning from Bad Experiences

Novelist James Baldwin commented, "Not everything that is faced can be changed. But nothing can be changed until it is faced." Often it takes a bad experience for us to face the changes we need to make in our lives. I know that was true for me when it came to my health. As I mentioned previously, I experienced a heart attack at age fifty-one. Prior to that, I knew deep down I wasn't eating right or exercising enough. But I'd never had any health problems, so I just plowed ahead as I always had. But the night I had the heart attack, the excruciating pain I felt in my chest and the belief in that moment that I wasn't going to see my family again finally got my attention. It made me face the fact that I needed to change the way I was living. You could say I had finally reached a teachable moment. And that is the value of the Law of Pain. It gives us an opportunity to turn our lives around. A bend in the road is not the end of the road unless you fail to make the turn.

> **A bend in the road is not the end of the road unless you fail to make the turn.**

Most people don't think their way to positive change—they feel their way. In their book, *The Heart of Change*, Harvard Business professor John Kotter and Deloitte Consulting principal Dan Cohen explain, "Changing behavior is less a matter of giving people analysis to influence their thoughts than helping them to see a truth to influence their feelings. Both thinking and feelings are essential, and both are found in successful organizations, but the heart of change is in the emotions."

When bad experiences create strong feelings in us, we either face the feelings and try to change or we try to escape. It's the old fight-or-flight instinct. We need to train ourselves to fight for positive changes. How do we do that? By remembering that our choices will lead to either the pain of self-discipline or the pain of regret. I'd rather live with the pain of self-discipline and reap the positive rewards than live with the pain of regret, which is something that can create a deep and continual ache within us.

Athlete and author Diana Nyad says, "I am willing to put myself through anything; temporary pain or discomfort means nothing to me as long as I can see that the experience will take me to a new level. I am interested in the unknown, and the only path to the unknown is through breaking barriers, an often-painful process." That's a process Nyad has gone through many times as she trained to break records as a long-distance swimmer. In 1979, she swam non-stop from Bimini in the Bahamas to Florida. It took her two days. Her record has stood for more than thirty years.

The next time you find yourself in the midst of a bad experience, remind yourself that you are on the cusp of an opportunity to change and grow. Whether you do will depend on how you react to your experience, and the changes you make as a result. Allow your emotions to be the catalyst for change, think through how to change to make sure you are making good choices, and then take action.

5. Take Responsibility for Your Life

Earlier I said that you need to recognize that your circumstances don't define you. They are outside of you and need not negatively impact your values and standards. At the same time, you must take responsibility for your life and the choices you make. Psychiatrist Frederic Flach, in his book *Resilience,* and psychologist Julius Segal, in *Winning Life's Toughest Battles,* indicate that people who overcome bad experiences avoid the label of "victim" and take responsibility for moving forward. They

> It's one short step from "why me" to "woe is me."

don't say, "What happened to me is the worst thing in the world, and I'll never be free of it." They say, "What happened to me was pretty bad, but other people are worse off, and I won't give up." They do not wallow in self-pity or ask, "Why me?" And that's a good thing, because it's one short step from "why me" to "woe is me."

It is nearly impossible to grow in any significant way when you don't take responsibility for yourself and your life. I remember an old song by comic singer Anna Russell that represents the attitude of many people in our culture today:

I went to my psychiatrist to be psychoanalyzed; To find out why I killed the cat and blackened my wife's eyes.

He put me on a downy couch, To see what he could
  find. And this is what he dredged up from my
  subconscious mind.
When I was one, my mommy hid my dolly in the
  trunk. And so it follows naturally that I am
  always drunk.
When I was two, I saw my father kiss the maid one
  day. And that is why I suffer now—kleptomania.
When I was three, I suffered from ambivalence
  toward my brothers. So it follows naturally, I
  poisoned all my lovers.
I'm so glad that I have learned the lesson it has
  taught: That everything I did that's wrong is
  someone else's fault.

In the last few years, I've done a lot of teaching and speaking in China. On a recent trip, the participants in a conference did a values exercise where people identify their top values using a pack of cards representing various values, such as integrity, independence, creativity, family, and so on. It's an exercise developed and used often by the John Maxwell Company. Thousands of people have done this activity, where they pick their top six values, then their top two, then their number one. What surprised me in China was the value most identified as number one: accountability. That says a lot about their culture.

No wonder they are making such strong advances in recent years.

No matter what you have gone through in your life—or what you are currently going through—you have the opportunity to grow from it. It's sometimes very difficult to see the opportunity in the midst of the pain, but it is there. You must be willing to not only look for it, but pursue it. As you do, perhaps the words of William Penn, English philosopher and founder of the Pennsylvania province, will encourage you: "No pain, no palm; no thorns, no throne; no gall, no glory; no cross, no crown."

Applying
the Law of Pain
to Your Life

1. Assess your attitude toward negative experiences up to this point in your life. Based on your personal history, which of the following statements best describes how you have approached failure, tragedy, problems, and challenges that have caused you pain?

- I do anything and everything possible to avoid pain at all costs.
- I know pain is inevitable, but I try to ignore it or block it out.
- I know everyone experiences pain, so I just endure it when it comes.
- I don't like pain, but I try to remain positive despite it.
- I process the emotion of painful experiences quickly and try to find a lesson in them.
- I process pain, find the lesson, and make changes proactively as a result.

Your goal should be to progress from wherever you are currently on the above scale to the place where you make positive changes in the wake of bad experiences.

2. In the past have you used bad experiences as a springboard for using your creativity? If not, use a current difficulty to help you learn how to become more creative by doing the following:

Define the problem.
Understand your emotion.
Articulate the lesson.
Identify a desired change.
Brainstorm numerous pathways.
Receive others' input.
Implement a course of action.

Remember, if you always do what you've always done, you'll always get what you've always gotten. If you want to arrive at a new destination, you need to take a new path.

3. No insight, no matter how profound, has value to you unless it is attached to changes that you will make based on what you've learned. Personal development requires a bias toward action!

Spend some time recalling the last five bad experiences you've had in your life. Write down each experience, along with what—if anything—you learned from it. Then evaluate whether you decided to make changes based on what you learned and rate yourself on how well you did at implementing those changes in your life. Once you've assessed each bad experience, give yourself a grade from A to F on how well you managed those experiences. If you haven't been an A or B student, you need to use the steps listed above to become better at the process.

9

The Law of the Ladder

Character Growth Determines the Height of Your Personal Growth

"Achievement to most people is something you do . . . to the high achiever, it is something you are."
—DOUG FIREBAUGH

Soon after I moved to Florida, I met Jerry Anderson. It didn't take long for us to become good friends. Jerry is a wonderful person and a very successful businessman. But he didn't start out that way. His story is a testament to how character growth determines personal growth and how personal growth leads to personal success.

Ambition without Guidance

Jerry grew up in Ohio and after graduating from high school, he began working in factories as a machinist and die maker. Though he was good at his trade, worked hard, and was successful, it wasn't enough for him. He was ambitious. He wanted to do more with his life than spend his career in a secure job and collect a gold watch when he retired. He wanted to be a success in business. So he left his factory job and set off on a career as an entrepreneur.

His first business venture involved selling precision tooling manufactured in Japan. The product was good, and Jerry knew his field, but the timing of the business wasn't optimal. This was in the early 1970s. At that time, the label "Made in Japan" wasn't seen as positive. Though Japanese manufacturing had come a long way since the years after World War II when the country had produced cheap goods, people in the United States hadn't yet recognized it, and they wouldn't buy the products. As a result, Jerry's first business failed.

Undaunted, Jerry wanted to try again. He changed strategies. This time he became part of a network marketing venture. Hardworking and ambitious, he poured his efforts into the new business. But this time everyone in the organization failed when the state investigated the organization and shut it down.

Even after that, Jerry was still determined not to give up. By this time he was living in California. He started a classified ad newspaper with a friend named Bernie Torrence. He also had interest in a franchise in Ohio that published a weekly real estate magazine. For three years, he gave the business everything he had, yet it was still failing.

Around that time, Jerry went to see John Schrock, a man Bernie looked up to and partnered with in business. Jerry asked John how he had managed to be so successful in his business dealings. John confided to him that he based his business dealings on values and principles.

"What values and principles?" Jerry asked.

"These," said John, taking a small, homemade book out of his jacket pocket. It contained sayings taken from the book of Proverbs and sorted by subject. John always carried it with him. "Anytime I have a business problem or question, I go to this book to get an answer."

John gave a copy of the little book to Jerry and encouraged him to use it.

To Be a Success, Think Like a Success

Jerry sensed that if he were to be a successful businessman, he needed to learn how to think like a successful businessman. With that in mind, he got together five or six other people and they committed to meet together once a week for an hour to study the principles in the little book John had given him. For the first time, he was intentional about his personal growth. And it didn't take long for his life and his business to change. The business, which had always struggled, turned around and for the first time made a profit. He expanded throughout the state of California and was so successful that the company was bought out.

Jerry moved back to Ohio to be closer to John. He did some consulting for a time, but it wasn't long before he wanted to start another business. Building on what he had already learned, he began working with another real estate magazine. In time, he grew it to be the largest publication of its kind in the United States, covering real estate in cities from Chicago to Miami and employing a thousand employees. Eventually, a company from New York bought him out again.

The Principles Start to Spread

By the 1980s, people who had heard about John Schrock were traveling to Ohio to meet him and learn from him. John had even written about some of his ideas and principles to try to help people. In the late 1980s, Jerry decided that he wanted to take the principles John had shared with him to the marketplace, and John and Bernie agreed to try it with him because they wanted to share what they had learned with others. They traveled around the United States, trying to interest businesspeople. They found few takers. But then they crossed paths with three men from Guatemala—a dentist, a corporate executive, and an owner of hardware stores—who were in Virginia looking for help with their businesses. When they saw the materials Jerry and his team had developed, they got excited and invited Jerry and his organization, which eventually became known as La Red, to come to Guatemala and help them.

Jerry's organization visited Guatemala City, and they were successful in launching roundtable groups very similar to the one that Jerry had started in California so many years before. The groups were encouraged to set a time to meet each week; discuss a principle, along with its characteristics and benefits;

evaluate themselves on where they stood in that area; and commit to taking specific action to change and improve it. The following week, they'd hold each other accountable for their commitments and then discuss the next principle. Over the course of a year, they would tackle these subjects:

Restraint	Boundaries	Ethics
Generosity	Proper Thinking	Ownership
Hard Work	Common Sense	Ambition
Motives	Prosperity	Listening
Honesty	Emotions	Co-Signing
Patience	Sowing	Responsibility
Humility	Direction	Debt
Productivity	Correction	Saving
Dependability	Conflict	Developing People
Temper	Pressure	Understanding People
Attitude	Criticism	Inspiration
Facts	Judgment	Influence
Goals	Confrontation	
Planning	Forgiveness	

Word got out about the success of what they were doing with businesspeople, and La Red was invited by the dean at a large university in Guatemala to teach values to the faculty, which at the time was known to take bribes and make other kinds of trades for grades. The values that were taught began to change the culture of the university, so much so that the university's board asked that all incoming freshmen be taught the same values. Today, between twelve and fifteen thousand students each year go through that course.

Not long after La Red was established in Guatemala, Jerry and his team were invited to Bogota, Colombia, to teach values again. They planned a launch where they expected about fifty people to show up. Instead there were hundreds and they had to move the meeting to a nearby city park.

As word spread in Colombia, representatives from the national government asked La Red to teach the same character principles to 11,500 government employees. Jerry happily accepted. Then he found out the employees were all prison guards. That was very intimidating. The prisons in Colombia were notoriously violent and corrupt. Incarcerated drug and guerilla leaders built suites for themselves in the prisons and ran their operations from them. Murders were a daily occurrence. And the administrators and guards at the prisons either went along with the corruption or were killed.

But the prisons were now being overseen by a general who had been coaxed out of retirement. A man with high integrity, General Cifuentes wanted to change the culture of the prisons, and he refused to turn a blind eye to the corruption. That determination cost the life of his son, who was mistakenly killed by hit men who thought he was the general.

And additional attempts were made on the general's life, but he survived them. He was the impetus for bringing Jerry into the prisons.

La Red introduced character development and values into 143 prisons holding seventy-five thousand prisoners, and the culture began to change. A year and a half later, the murder rate was down dramatically. And there were reports that some of the prisoners actually said they wanted to be more like the guards. Certainly, the prisons had not become pleasant places, but they had changed. And that prompted the Colombian military to ask that La Red begin training military troops in character development.

La Red continues to take character values and principles to businesses, governments, education, and churches around the globe. Currently they are helping people in forty-four nations. They estimate that more than one million people have been trained in a foundation of values-based principles. And that's important, because character growth determines the height of your personal growth. And without personal growth, you can never reach your potential.

The Value of Character

Professors James Kouzes and Barry Posner have spent more than twenty-five years surveying leaders in virtually every type of organization, in which they ask, "What values, personal traits, or characteristics do you look for and admire in a leader?" During those years, they have administered a survey questionnaire called "Characteristics of Admired Leaders" to more than seventy-five thousand people on six continents: Africa, North America, South America, Asia, Europe, and Australia.[1] "The results," they report, "have been striking in their regularity over the years, and they do not significantly vary by demographical, organizational, or cultural differences." And what quality is most admired in leaders? The answer is honesty.

As Kouzes and Posner explain, honesty, which is the core of good character, is the quality that most enhances or damages personal reputations. They write,

> In almost every survey conducted, honesty has been selected more often than any other leadership characteristic; overall, it emerges as the single most important factor in the leader-constituent relationships. The percentages vary, but the final ranking does not. From the first time we conducted our studies honesty has been at the top of the list.[2]

It comes as little surprise that people want to follow leaders of good character. No one likes to work

> "In almost every survey conducted, honesty has been selected more often than any other leadership characteristic."
>
> —James Kouzes and Barry Posner

with unreliable people. But before you or I work with any other person or follow any other leader, who do we have to rely on every day? Ourselves! That's why character is so important. If you cannot trust yourself, you won't ever be able to grow. Good character, with honesty and integrity at its core, is essential to success in any area of life. Without it, a person is building on shifting sand.

Bill Thrall asserts that people often focus on their professional capacity without developing character, and it almost always costs them in the end. It costs them their personal relationships and often their career. He likens it to climbing a long extension ladder that lacks the proper support. The higher a person climbs, the more wobbly and unstable it can become, until the person climbing it finally falls.[3]

Retired general Norman Schwarzkopf asserted, "Ninety-nine percent of leadership failures are failures of character." So are ninety-nine percent of all other failures. Most people focus too much on competence and too little on character. How often does a person miss a deadline because he didn't follow through when he should have? How many times do people get lower grades on tests than they could have because they didn't study as much as they should have? How frequently do people fail to grow not because they didn't have time to read help-

> "Ninety-nine percent of leadership failures are failures of character."
>
> —*Norman Schwarzkopf*

ful books but because they chose to spend their time and money on something else that was less worthwhile? All of those shortcomings are the result of character, not capacity. Character growth determines the height of your personal growth. That's the Law of the Ladder.

Rungs on My Character Ladder

Climbing the ladder of character is something that I have always had to do intentionally. It doesn't just happen for me. It probably doesn't just happen for you either. It's taken me decades to develop the right mind-set and learn what "rungs" need to be in place in order for me to improve. Here are the ones on my character ladder that have empowered me to climb higher. Perhaps they will also help you to climb.

1. I Will Focus on Being Better on the Inside than on the Outside—Character Matters

I believe it is a normal human desire to be concerned about how we look on the outside. There's nothing wrong with that. What can get us in trouble is worrying more about how we look on the outside than about how we really are on the inside. Our reputation comes from what others believe about our outside. Our character represents who we are on the inside. And the good news is that if you focus on being better on the inside than on the outside, over time you will also become better on the outside. Why do I say that?

THE INSIDE INFLUENCES THE OUTSIDE

More than twenty-five hundred years ago, the Proverbs writer noted that as we think in our hearts, so we become.[4] That ancient idea has been both echoed by other wisdom writers and confirmed by modern science. Coaches teach the importance of visualization for winning. Psychologists point out the power of self-image on people's actions. Doctors note the impact of positive attitude and hope on healing.

What we believe really matters. We reap what we sow. What we do or neglect to do in the privacy of our daily lives impacts who we are. If you neglect your heart, mind, and soul, it changes who you are on the outside as well as on the inside.

INSIDE VICTORIES PRECEDE OUTSIDE ONES

If you do the things you need to do when you need to do them, then someday you can do the things you want to do when you want to do them. In other words, before you can *do*, you must *be*.

> If you do the things you need to do when you need to do them, then someday you can do the things you want to do when you want to do them.

I have often observed people who seemed to be doing all the right things on the outside, yet they were not experiencing success. When that happens, I usually conclude that something is wrong on the inside and needs to be changed. The right motions outwardly with wrong motives inwardly will not bring lasting progress. Right outward talking with wrong inward thinking will not bring lasting success. Expressions of care on the outside with a heart of hatred or contempt on the inside will not bring lasting peace. Continual growth and lasting success are the result of aligning the inside and the outside of our lives. And getting the inside right must come first—with solid character traits that provide the foundation for growth.

Our Inside Development Is Totally within Our Control

We often cannot determine what happens to us, but we can always determine what happens within us. Jim Rohn said,

Character is a quality that embodies many important traits such as integrity, courage, perseverance, confidence, and wisdom. Unlike your fingerprints that you were born with and can't change, character is something that you create within yourself and must take responsibility for changing.

When we fail to make the right character choices within us, we give away ownership of ourselves. We belong to others—to whatever gains control of us. And that puts us in a bad place. How can you ever reach your potential and become the person you can be if others are making your choices for you?

The "rungs" on my character ladder have come as the result of hard-fought personal choices. They were not easily made and they are not easily managed. Every day there is a battle from the outside for me to compromise or surrender them. Regretfully, there have been times when I have. But whenever that's happened, I have diligently gone after them to return them to their respectful place... inside of me.

Doug Firebaugh, author and multilevel marketing expert, says, "Winning in life is more than just money... it's about winning on the inside... and knowing that you have played the game of life with all you had... and then some." If you want to be successful, you must prioritize building your inside ahead of your outside.

Several years ago, teenage millionaire phenomenon Farrah Gray wrote a book called *Reallionaire*. He coined the term to describe "someone who has discovered that there is more to money than having money. A person who understands that success is not just about being rich in your pocket; you have to be rich on the inside, too." At a tender age, he recognized that money without a strong character foundation can lead not to success but to ruin. If you have any doubt, just look at the number of famous child actors and young pop stars who have crashed and burned. Their stories are often sad because they focused on the externals of life instead of building internally to give themselves a strong foundation when fame and fortune came. Theirs is a fate we need to work hard to avoid by focusing on improving on the inside more than on the outside.

2. I Will Follow the Golden Rule—People Matter

Several years ago when I was asked to write a book on ethics in business, the result was *Ethics 101,* which I based on the golden rule. If you had to pick only one guideline for life, you couldn't do better than this: "Here is a simple, rule-of-thumb guide for behavior: Ask yourself what you want people to do for you,

> "Here is a simple, rule-of-thumb guide for behavior: Ask yourself what you want people to do for you, then grab the initiative and do it for them."
>
> —THE MESSAGE

then grab the initiative and do it for them."[5]

Following the golden rule is a wonderful character builder. It prompts you to focus on other people. It leads you to be empathetic. It encourages you to take the high road. And if you stick to it—especially when it's difficult—you can't help but become the kind of person others want to be around. After all, in the end in all of our relationships we are either plusses or minuses in the lives of others. The golden rule helps us to remain a plus.

3. I Will Teach Only What I Believe—Passion Matters

Most speakers are asked early in their careers to talk about a wide variety of subjects. Or they come from a particular tradition that expects them to weigh in on certain topics from a particular point of view. For example, motivational speakers are often expected to proclaim, "If you believe it, you can achieve it."

> Borrowed beliefs have no passion, therefore no power.

When I was first starting out in my career, there were a few things I taught that I didn't buy into a hundred percent.

I'm not talking about things that are clearly right or wrong. I'm talking about subjective things that are a matter of opinion. But as soon as I spoke about them, I regretted it.

Do you know what they call a speaker who teaches what he doesn't believe? A hypocrite! So early on, I vowed to teach only what I believe. And that has benefitted me, not only in the area of integrity, but also in the area of passion. Borrowed beliefs have no passion, therefore no power. Some of the things I was passionate about thirty years ago, such as the effectiveness of learning REAL—relationships, equipping, attitude, and leadership—I'm still just as passionate about today. And if anything, I'm even more passionate today about the statement "everything rises and falls on leadership" than I was when I first communicated it to an audience.

Individuals who lack principles and passion become beige people. I don't ever want to become one of those. I bet you don't want to either.

4. I Will Value Humility Above All Virtues—Perspective Matters

Playwright and author J. M. Barrie observed, "The life of every man is a diary in which he means to write one story and writes another; and his humblest hour is when he compares the volume as it is with what he

> "The life of every man is a diary in which he means to write one story and writes another; and his humblest hour is when he compares the volume as it is with what he hoped to make it."
>
> —J. M. Barrie

hoped to make it." I think anyone who is honest with himself realizes that he falls short of where he could and should be in life. Unlike what Tom Hanks said as Forrest Gump, life is not a box of chocolates. It's more like a jar of jalapeños. What we do today might burn our butts tomorrow!

We don't intend to make mistakes and to fall short, but we do. We're all just one step away from stupid. Author, pastor, and friend Andy Stanley says, "I've concluded that while nobody plans to mess up their life, the problem is that few of us plan not to. That is, we don't put the necessary safeguards in place to ensure a happy ending."

So how do we do that?

REMEMBER THE BIG PICTURE

I think the first thing to do is remind ourselves of the big picture. It's said that President John F. Kennedy kept a small plaque in the White House with the inscription "Oh God, thy sea is so great and my boat is so small." If the person known as the leader of the free world can keep perspective of his true place in the world, so should we.

RECOGNIZE THAT EVERYONE HAS WEAKNESSES

Rick Warren gives good advice about how to remain humble. He suggests admitting our weaknesses, being patient with others' weaknesses, and being open to correction. Of those three things, I have to admit that I do only one of them fairly well. I don't find it difficult to admit my weaknesses—maybe because I have so many. I have a much harder time being patient with others. I am constantly having to remind myself to extend grace to others. And in order to be more open to correction, I never assume that I will not mess up, I develop relationships with good people who will speak the truth to me, and I set up accountability systems in my life.

BE TEACHABLE

I love being around people who have a beginner's mind-set. They think of themselves as apprentices instead of experts and, as a result, have a humble, teachable posture. They try to see things from others' perspective. They are open to new ideas. They possess a thirst for knowledge. They ask questions and know how to listen. And they gather as much information as possible before making decisions. I admire such people and try to be like them.

BE WILLING TO SERVE OTHERS

Few things are better for cultivating character and developing humility than serving others. Putting others first right-sizes our egos and perspective. (If you are a leader, then you especially need to remember this because you can get used to being served by others and come to think you are entitled to it.)

In their book *Winning: The Answers*, Jack and Suzy Welch describe people who "swell" because of their success and as a result develop the wrong kind of attitude toward others. They write,

> People who swell develop all sorts of unappealing behaviors. They're arrogant, especially toward their peers and subordinates. They hoard credit and belittle the efforts of others, don't share ideas except to show them off, and don't listen very well, if at all. Bosses can spot these team-killing behaviors a mile away, and so it is no wonder that those with "power and authority" around you, as you put it, have consistently worked against you. You may be very smart and deliver stellar results on the job, but your swollen personality is the kind that undermines the morale in any organization and ultimately can really damage performance.[6]

How does a person who is used to winning remind himself that it's not all about him? By serving others. For me, service starts with Margaret and the rest of my family. Also, beginning in 1997, I've selected a handful of individuals every year who I can try to serve without receiving anything in return. And I also look for ways to serve my team, since they work so hard to serve me and our vision every day.

BE GRATEFUL

I am very conscious of the fact that I have been blessed and don't deserve what I've received in life. I am indebted to God and others, and because of that, I try to maintain an attitude of gratitude. That isn't always easy. Consultant Fred Smith, who mentored me for many years, helped me in this area. He said, "We do not stay grateful because that makes us indebted, and we don't want to be indebted. The biblical phrase 'sacrifice of thanksgiving' was a puzzle to me until I realized that gratitude is acknowledging that someone did something for me that I could not do for myself. Gratitude expresses our vulnerability, our dependence on others."

A Chinese proverb says that those who drink the water must remember those who dug the well. Everything

> Those who drink the water must remember those who dug the well.

we do, every accomplishment we have, every milestone we pass has come in part because of the efforts of others. There are no self-made men or women. If we can remember that, we can be grateful. And if we are grateful, we are more likely to develop good character than if we aren't.

Confucius asserted, "Humility is the solid foundation of all the virtues." In other words, it paves the way for character growth. And that sets us up for personal growth. These things are definitely connected.

5. I Will Strive to Finish Well—Faithfulness Matters

The final "rung" on my character ladder is the determination to keep building character and living at the highest standard until the day I die. I am endeavoring to do that by doing the right thing and becoming a better person every day. To do the right thing, I don't wait to feel like it. I recognize that emotion follows motion. Do the right thing and you feel right. Do the wrong thing and you feel bad. If you take control of your behavior, your emotions will fall into place.

> If you take control of your behavior, your emotions will fall into place.

Pastor and radio broadcaster Tony Evans says, "If you want a better world, composed of better nations, inhabited by better states, filled with better counties, made up of better cities, comprised of better neighborhoods, illuminated by better churches, populated by better families, then you'll have to start by becoming a better person." That's always where it starts—with me, with you. If we focus on personal character, we make the world a better place. If we do that our entire lives, we've done the best thing we can do to improve our world.

The Stronger Your Character, the Greater Your Growth Potential

Pulitzer Prize–winning author Alexander Solzhenitsyn spent eight years in prison during the Soviet era for criticizing Joseph Stalin. He went into prison an atheist and came out a person of faith. The experience didn't leave him bitter. It left him grateful for the development of his faith and the strengthening of his character. Looking back on the experience, he said, "I bless you, prison—I bless you for being in my life—for there lying on rotting prison straw, I learned the object of life is not prospering as I had grown up believing, but the maturing of the soul."

If we desire to grow and reach our potential, we must pay more attention to our character than to our success. We must recognize that personal growth means more than expanding our minds and adding to our skills. It means increasing our capacity as human beings. It means maintaining core integrity, even when it hurts. It means being who we should be, not just being where we want to be. It means maturing our souls.

Physician and author Orison Swett Marden once described a successful person by saying, "He was born mud and died marble. This gives us an interesting metaphor to use to look at various lives. Some people are born mud and remain mud. . . . Sadly, some are born marble and die mud; some are born mud, dream of marble, but remain mud. But many persons of high character have been born mud and died marble." Isn't that a wonderful thought? I hope that can be said of me at the end of my life, and I hope the same for you.

Applying
the Law of the Ladder
to Your Life

1. Assess where you have put most of your focus up until this point in your life. Has it been on improving on the inside or on the outside? Here are some of the ways you can do that: Compare how much you spent in the last twelve months on clothing, jewelry, accessories, and so on, versus how much you spent on books, conferences, and that sort of thing. Compare how much time you spent in the last month on personal and spiritual growth versus activities related to appearance. If you exercise regularly, examine what benefits you are striving for: Do they relate to inner health or outer appearance?

If your assessment reveals more of an outward focus than an inward one, then determine how to shift your focus by adding time, money, and attention to the things that will make you grow even if they do not show.

2. Plan to spend time in the coming months to regularly serve others. Putting aside your own agenda

and putting others first will help you to develop humility, character, and others-mindedness. Start with your family if you aren't in the habit of doing things for them.

Another idea is to set aside at least an hour every week for volunteering. Schedule it, and then give it a hundred percent of your focus while you're serving.

3. U.S. Senator Dan Coats said, "Character cannot be summoned at the moment of crisis if it has been squandered by years of compromise and rationalization. The only testing ground for the heroic is the mundane. The only preparation for that one profound decision which can change a life, or even a nation, is those hundreds of half-conscious, self-defining, seemingly insignificant decisions made in private. Habit is the daily battleground of character."

> "Habit is the daily battleground of character."
>
> —Dan Coats

What are you doing every day to develop the habit of character growth? Are you giving attention to your soul? Are you doing hard or unpleasant things? Are you practicing the golden rule and putting others ahead of yourself? Your character isn't set. You can improve it. It's never too late. You can change who you are and your overall potential by becoming a better person.

10

The Law of the Rubber Band

Growth Stops When You Lose the Tension Between Where You Are and Where You Could Be

"Only a mediocre person is always at his best."
—W. Somerset Maugham

When I was a kid growing up, I loved sports and I was a pretty decent athlete. I discovered basketball in fourth grade, and it became my passion. I played it through high school. Like most kids in college, I was active and pretty fit. And in my twenties, I continued to play pick-up basketball games with friends and added golf to my routine. But as I went farther in my career and got into my thirties and forties, I didn't exercise and take care of my health as I should have. I paid for that when I was fifty-one and suffered a heart attack.

Since that time, exercise has been a regular part of my routine. For many years I walked or ran on a treadmill. I'd sometimes run part of the golf course when playing with friends. About five years ago, I switched to swimming, attempting to put in an hour of exercise every day in the pool. More recently, I've begun doing Pilates with Margaret. These exercises focus primarily on building core muscle strength and flexibility. To achieve that flexibility, there is an emphasis on physical stretching. We've found it to be very beneficial and rewarding. I believe I'm currently in the best shape I've been in thirty-five years.

A Series of Stretches

As I prepared to write this chapter, I was reminded of all the professional stretching I've had to do over the course of my career. One of my favorite quotes, which I collected as a teenager says, "God's gift to us: potential. Our gift to God: developing it." How do we do that? By getting out of our comfort zone. By continually stretching—not only physically but also mentally, emotionally, and spiritually.

> "God's gift to us: potential. Our gift to God: developing it."
> —Author unknown

Life begins at the end of our comfort zone. We go there by stretching.

When I look back on the last forty years or so, I can see that much of the progress I've had in my career has come as the result of stretching experiences. Take a look at some of them that follow.

Choosing My First Pastorate

I went to a church where no one knew my dad, who was a district superintendent. My start was slower than it undoubtedly would have been if I'd gone somewhere Dad could have helped me. As it was, I had to work harder than I might have otherwise. And I had to find myself and learn what I was really capable of.

I believe this helped to define my career. I was determined to work hard and be creative in finding ways to lead people and grow my church. I learned so many leadership lessons in that first church. And I learned how to love people better.

Focusing on Teaching Leadership

When I started talking about leadership in the midseventies, it was a topic other pastors were not talking about. There were people who criticized me for focusing on what they considered a "secular" message, though I have to say I find that peculiar, since the greatest leaders of all time can be found in the Bible: Abraham, Moses, David, Jesus, and Paul, just to name a few. Even forty years later, some continue to criticize me for it.

So why did I keep teaching it? Because pastors are required to lead people, and in my day, they received no training in leadership, even though they must do it every day of their careers. Early on, I struggled as a leader. I knew others would too. I wanted to help them. By stretching through this experience, I was not only able to help many pastors, but I was able to discover the message that I believe I was born to teach.

Learning to Communicate Internationally

I remember the first time I spoke using an interpreter. It was in Japan. The process was uncomfortable because I had to say a phrase or two, pause for what I said to be translated, and then say a bit more, pause again, and so on. And of course there are many cultural differences that need to be bridged. I found it difficult. After I had finished speaking, Margaret said that our daughter, Elizabeth, who was eight years old at the time, leaned over to her at one point and said, "Dad's not very good, is he?" Even a child could tell that I was not connecting well with my audience.

I enjoy communicating, and the easiest thing for me to do would have been to simply give up the idea of speaking to others outside of the United States. I had already learned how to communicate effectively in English. However, I saw this as an opportunity to stretch and grow—and maybe someday make a greater impact. It took me almost a decade to learn how to connect with people in other cultures while working with a translator, but it's definitely been worth it. That groundwork made it possible for me to start EQUIP, which now trains leaders in 175 countries around the world.

Crossing Over to a New Audience

After I had been teaching leadership to pastors for about ten years, I began to notice a trend. More and more businesspeople were attending my leadership conferences. I welcomed this, because I had been teaching leadership to laypeople as well as staff in my own church for years. But it didn't prompt me to change what I was doing. Then one day, when I was meeting with my publisher, I learned that my books were being purchased more and more through secular retailers rather than religious ones. In fact, over the course of time, it had shifted so that two-thirds of the sales were through regular retail channels.

I saw this as an incredible opportunity to reach many more people than I otherwise would. But there was a challenge. Could I connect and communicate with businesspeople? People expect one thing when they sit in a church to hear a message from a pastor. They expect something entirely different when they pay money to hear a speaker. I wasn't sure whether I would be able to succeed. It was another stretching experience.

Focusing on Building a Legacy

When I turned sixty, I was prepared to slow down. I had moved to a sunny, warm climate, which I loved. I was financially blessed. I had grandchildren, which is the most wonderful gift a person can have in this life. I would continue to write and speak, but not at the pace I had before. It was a season of harvest after decades of work.

But then some opportunities presented themselves. My books were now with a new publisher. I was approached about starting a coaching company. And I had the chance to regain control of the training and development materials I had created over the previous decade. What would I do?

It would mean stretching again, but I was willing to seize the opportunity—and accept the challenge. And I'm so glad I did. I have entered another season of sowing, instead of just harvesting. I believe it will allow me to help many more people than I would have if I'd simply slowed down.

The Benefits of Tension

Many years ago, during one of the sessions I taught at a leadership conference, I put a rubber band on the table at the place of every attendee. Then I started the session by asking about all the ways people could think of for using them. At the end of the discussion time, I asked them if they could identify the one thing all of their uses had in common. Maybe you've already guessed what it was. Rubber bands are useful only when they are stretched! That can also be said of us.

1. Few People Want to Stretch

There's a joke about a longtime handyman named Sam who was once offered a full-time job by a mill owner who was having problems with muskrats at the mill's dam. The owner asked Sam to rid the mill of the pests and even provided a rifle for him to do the job.

Sam was ecstatic because it was the first steady work with a regular paycheck that he'd ever gotten.

One day, several months later, a friend came to visit Sam. He found him sitting on a grassy bank, the gun across his knees.

"Hey, Sam. Whatcha doin'?" he asked.

"My job, guarding the dam."

"From what?"

"Muskrats."

His friend looked over at the dam, and just at that moment a muskrat appeared.

"There's one!" the friend exclaimed. "Shoot him!"

Sam didn't move. Meanwhile, the muskrat scurried away.

"Why the heck didn't you shoot him?"

"Are you crazy?" replied Sam. "Do you think I want to lose my job?"

You may think that joke is silly, but it's much closer to the truth than we may like to admit. I say that because when I was in college, one of the jobs I had was at a local meat-packing plant. My job was to haul racks of meat to the refrigeration units and get orders for customers, but I was curious about the whole operation and wanted to understand how it worked. After I'd been there a couple of weeks, Pense, a worker who'd been there for many years, took me aside and said, "You ask too many questions. The less you know, the less you have to do." His job was to kill cows at the plant. And that's all he ever wanted to do. He was like the character in a *Wall Street Journal* cartoon I saw who told the personnel manager, "I know I'm overqualified, but I promise to use only half my ability."

Most people use only a small fraction of their ability and rarely strive to reach their full potential. There is no tension to grow in their lives, little desire to stretch. Sadly, a third of high school graduates never read another book for the rest of their

> **Forty-two percent of college graduates never read a book after college.**

lives, and 42 percent of college graduates similarly never read a book after college.[1] And publisher David Godine claims that only 32 percent of the U.S. population has ever been in a bookstore.[2] I don't know if people are aware of the gap between where they are and where they could be, but relatively few seem to be reading books to try to close it.

Too many people are willing to settle for average in life. Is that bad? Read this description written by Edmund Gaudet, and then you decide:

"Average" is what the failures claim to be when their family and friends ask them why they are not more successful.

"Average" is the top of the bottom, the best of the worst, the bottom of the top, the worst of the best. Which of these are you?

"Average" means being run-of-the-mill, mediocre, insignificant, an also-ran, a nonentity.

Being "average" is the lazy person's cop-out; it's lacking the guts to take a stand in life; it's living by default.

Being "average" is to take up space for no purpose; to take the trip through life, but never to pay the fare; to return no interest for God's investment in you.

Being "average" is to pass one's life away with time, rather than to pass one's time away with life; it's to kill time, rather than to work it to death.

To be "average" is to be forgotten once you pass from this life. The successful are remembered for their contributions; the failures are remembered because they tried; but the "average," the silent majority, is just forgotten.

To be "average" is to commit the greatest crime one can against one's self, humanity, and one's God. The saddest epitaph is this: "Here lies Mr. and Ms. Average—here lies the remains of what might have been, except for their belief that they were only "average."[3]

I cannot stand the idea of settling for average, can you? Nobody admires average. The best organizations don't pay for average. Mediocrity is not worth shooting for. As novelist Arnold Bennett said, "The real tragedy is the tragedy of the man who never in his life braces himself for his one supreme effort, who never stretches to his full capacity, never stands up to his full stature." We must be aware of the gap that stands between us and our potential, and let the tension of that gap motivate us to keep striving to become better.

2. Settling for the Status Quo Ultimately Leads to Dissatisfaction

I believe most people are naturally tempted to settle into a comfort zone where they choose comfort over potential. They fall into familiar patterns and habits, doing the same things in the same ways with the same people at the same time and getting the same results. It's true that being in your comfort zone may feel good, but it leads to mediocrity and, therefore, dissatisfaction. As psychologist Abraham Maslow asserted, "If you plan on being anything less than you are capable of being, you will probably be unhappy all the days of your life."

> "If you plan on being anything less than you are capable of being, you will probably be unhappy all the days of your life."
>
> —Abraham Maslow

If you have ever settled for the status quo and then wondered why your life isn't going the way you'd hoped, then you need to realize that you will only reach your potential if you have the courage to push yourself outside your comfort zone and break out of a mind-set of mediocrity. You must be willing to leave behind what feels familiar, safe, and secure. You must give up excuses and push forward. You must be willing to face the tension that comes from stretching toward your potential. That is the only way to avoid what poet John Greenleaf Whittier described when he wrote, "For all sad words of tongue or pen, the saddest are these: 'It might have been.'"

3. Stretching Always Starts from the Inside Out

When I was a teenager, my dad asked me to read *As a Man Thinketh* by James Allen. It had a profound impact on my life. It made me realize that reaching your potential started on the inside. Allen wrote, "Your circumstances may be uncongenial, but they shall not long remain so if you but perceive an ideal and strive to reach it. You cannot travel within and stand still without."

> "You cannot travel within and stand still without."
> —James Allen

Most people have a dream. For some, it's on the tip of their tongue, and for others, it's buried deep in their hearts, but everyone has one. However, not very many people are pursuing it. When I teach on the subject of achieving a dream, and I ask the audience how many have a dream, nearly everyone raises his hand. When I ask, "How many are pursuing that dream?" fewer than half raise their hands. And when the question is, "How many are achieving their dream?" I see only a few scattered hands being raised.

What is stopping them? For that matter, what is stopping you? The authors of *Now Discover Your Strengths*, Marcus Buckingham and Donald O. Clifton, cite Gallup polls indicating that most people don't like their current jobs, yet they don't make a change. What's stopping them? Most Americans want to lose weight, but they don't make the effort to do so. I run across people all the time who tell me that they want to write a book, but when I ask, "Have you started writing?" the answer is almost always no. Instead of wishing, wanting, and waiting, people need to search inside themselves for reasons to start.

It's wise to remember that our situation in life is mainly due to the choices we make and the actions we do—or fail to—take. The older we are, the more responsible we are for our situation. If you are merely average or if you are no closer to your dream this year than you were last year, you can choose to accept it, defend it, cover it up, and explain it away. Or you can choose to change it, grow from it, and forge a new path.

Jim Rohn observed, "Every life form seems to strive to its maximum except human beings. How tall will a tree grow? As tall as it possibly can. Human beings, on the other hand, have been given the dignity of choice. You can choose to be all or you can choose to be less. Why not stretch up to the full measure of the challenge and see what all you can do?"

Where do you find the internal impetus for stretching? Measure what you're doing against what you're capable of. Measure yourself against yourself. Make a contest of it. If you have no idea what you might be capable of, talk to people who care about you and believe in you. Don't have any people in your life who fit that description? Then go look for some. Find a mentor who can help you see yourself for who you *could* be, not who you currently are. And then use that image to inspire you to start stretching.

4. Stretching Always Requires Change

At the beginning of this chapter I wrote about my five major professional stretching experiences. As I reflect upon these times in my life, I have to admit that it was a challenge to change. I didn't like it. I like being comfortable and am always tempted to resist stretching. But growth doesn't come from staying in your comfort zone. You can't improve and avoid change at the same time. So how do I embrace change and kick myself out of my comfort zone?

First of all, I stop looking over my shoulder. It's difficult to focus on your past and change in the present. That's why for years I had on my desk a little plaque that said, "Yesterday ended last night." It helped me to focus on the present and work to improve what I could *today*. That's important. Author and contributor to the *Chicken Soup for the Soul* series Alan Cohen says, "To grow, you must be willing to let your present and future be totally unlike your past. Your history is not your destiny."

The second thing I do is work to develop my "reach muscle." A. G. Buckham, who pioneered aviation photography in the early days of flight,

> "Monotony is the awful reward of the careful."
> —A. G. Buckham

observed, "Monotony is the awful reward of the careful." If you want to grow and change, you must take risks.

Innovation and progress are often initiated by people who push for change. *Jeopardy!* host Alex Trebek observed, "Have you ever met a successful person who wasn't restless—who was satisfied with where he or she was in life? They want new challenges. They want to get up and go . . . and that's one of the reasons they're successful."

It's unfortunate that the word *entrepreneur* has come to mean *gambler* to some people. But risk has advantages. People who take risks learn more and faster than those who don't. Their depth and range of experience is often greater. And they learn how to solve problems. All of those help a person to grow.

> "It's never too late to be what you might have been."
> —*George Elliot*

The greatest stretching seasons of life come when we do what we have never done, push ourselves harder, and reach in a way that is uncomfortable to us. That takes courage. But the good news is that it causes us to grow in ways we thought were impossible. And it gives life to what novelist George Elliot said: "It's never too late to be what you might have been."

5. Stretching Sets You Apart from Others

America seems to be increasingly satisfied with mediocrity. Yet it isn't at its root a national problem; it's a personal concession to do less than our best. It takes an individual to say, "I guess good enough is good enough." But unfortunately, mediocrity spreads from person to person and eventually metastasizes until an entire nation is at risk.

Excellence seems to be moving farther and farther from the norm. However, people who live by the Law of the Rubber Band and use the tension between where they are and where they could be as impetus to stretch can distinguish themselves from their peers.

Jack and Suzy Welch address this issue in their book *Winning: The Answers* when a young person entering the corporate world asks, "How can I quickly distinguish myself as a winner?" They answer,

First of all, forget some of the most basic habits you learned in school. Once you are in the real world—and it doesn't matter if you are twenty-two or sixty-two, starting your first job or your fifth—the way to get ahead is to over-deliver.

Look, for years, you've been taught the virtues of meeting specific expectations. And you've been trained that it's an A-plus performance to fully answer every question the teacher asks.

Those days are over. To get an A-plus in business you have to expand the organization's expectations of you and then exceed them, and you have to fully answer every question the "teacher" asks, *plus* a slew of questions he or she didn't even think of.

Your goal, in other words, should be to make your bosses smarter, your team more effective, and the whole company more competitive because of your energy, creativity, and insights....

If your boss asks you for a report on the outlook of one of your company's products over the next year, you can be sure she already has a solid sense of the answer. So, go beyond being the grunt assigned to confirm her hunch. Do the extra research, legwork, and data crunching to give her something that really expands her thinking. . . .

In other words, give your boss something that shocks and awes her, something new and interesting that she can report to *her* bosses. In time, those kinds of ideas will move the company forward and you upward.

Improving yourself is the best way to help your team. Successful people set themselves apart because they initiate the improvement others need. When you get better, those around you benefit. Excellence has the potential to spread in the same way that mediocrity does. The positives or negatives of a group always begin with one. When you get better, so will others.

6. Stretching Can Become a Lifestyle

When we stop stretching, I believe we stop really living. We may keep on breathing. Our vital life signs may be working. But we are dead on the inside and dead to our greatest possibilities. As editor James Terry White observed, "Nature has everywhere written her protest against idleness; everything which ceases to struggle, which remains inactive, rapidly deteriorates. It is the struggle toward an ideal, the constant effort to get higher and further, which develops manhood and character."

I'm getting older. I will not always be able to perform at my peak level. But I intend to keep reading, asking questions, talking to interesting people, working hard, and exposing myself to new experiences until I die. Too many people are dead but just haven't made it official yet! Rabbi Nachman of Bratslav said, "If you won't be better tomorrow than you were today, then what do you need tomorrow for?" I refuse to give up growing. The following words sum up how I feel:

I'm not where I'm supposed to be,
I'm not what I want to be,
But I'm not what I used to be.
I haven't learned how to arrive;
I've just learned how to keep going.

I'm going to keep on stretching until I'm all stretched out. And it doesn't matter whether I see success today or not. Why? Because, sadly, many people stop growing after they have tasted success. Management expert Peter Drucker observed, "The greatest enemy of tomorrow's success is today's success. No one has ever made a significant impact after they

> "If you won't be better tomorrow than you were today, then what do you need tomorrow for?"
> —Rabbi Nachman of Bratslav

won the Nobel Prize." I don't want success, no matter how great or small, to derail me.

7. Stretching Gives You a Shot at Significance

Indian statesman Mahatma Gandhi stated, "The difference between what we do and what we are capable of doing would suffice to solve most of the world's problems." That difference is the gap between good and great. And what closes the gap is our willingness to stretch.

People who exist on the "good" side of the gap live in the land of the permissible. What they do is okay. They follow the rules and don't make waves. But do they make the difference they could if they followed the Law of the Rubber Band? Cross over the gap and you find yourself on the "great" side. That is the land of the possible. It's where people achieve in extraordinary fashion. They do more than they believed they were capable of, and they make an impact. How? By continually focusing on making the next stretch. They continually leave their comfort zone and stretch toward their capacity zone.

> "A possibility is a hint from God. One must follow it."
> —Søren Kierkegaard

Philosopher Søren Kierkegaard said, "A possibility is a hint from God. One must follow it." That possibility path is God giving us an opportunity to make a difference. As we follow it we stop asking ourselves what we are, and we start asking what can we become. We may appreciate what we did yesterday, but we don't put it on a pedestal. It looks small in comparison to the possibilities in the future. Looking forward fills us with energy. We resonate with the words of Robert Louis Stevenson, who said, "To be what we are, and to become what we are capable of becoming, is the only end in life."

Significance is birthed within each of us. If we are willing to stretch, that seed can grow until it begins to bear fruit in our lives. What's fantastic is that the change within us challenges us to make changes around us, and our growth creates a belief in us that others can grow. When that happens in an environment and everybody is stretching and growing, then indifference is replaced with make-a-difference. And that's how we begin to change our world.

Stretching to the End

One of my favorite sports heroes is Ted Williams, said to be the greatest hitter in the history of Major League Baseball. The last man to bat over .400 in a season, he retired with 521 home runs and a career batting average of .344. It's said that Williams could heft a bat and tell the difference between his normal thirty-four-ounce bat and one weighing half an ounce less. He once complained about the way the handles of a bunch of bats felt and sent them back. It turned out that their thickness was five-thousandths of an inch off. And when he watched a ball coming toward him as he stood at bat, he could tell what kind of pitch it was by the way the laces moved. The man loved hitting baseballs and was meticulous about every aspect of it. And for as long as he lived he was constantly learning and continuing to stretch in this area.

I recently read an anecdote about a meeting between Williams and Boston Celtics coach Red Auerbach in the 1950s. As the two greats discussed their sports, Williams asked, "What do your guys eat on the day of a game?"

"What do you want to know for?" Auerbach replied. "You seem to be doing all right with what you're doing."

"I'm always looking for new ways to improve what I do."

Auerbach said of Williams, "He thought of the little things, what's important to being great. When you're great and you excel, some athletes would coast on that.... Here's the best hitter in baseball, and he's trying to get another little percentage point."

As much as any athlete I've ever read about, Williams lived by the Law of the Rubber Band. He understood that growth stops when you lose the tension between where you are and where you could be. For most people, as time goes by they lose the tension that prompts growth—especially if they experience any success. But having less tension makes people less productive. And it undermines the growth toward their potential. Remarkably, when it came to hitting, Williams never lost that tension. Long after he retired from baseball, he still talked about hitting with anyone who cared about it. He was continually learning—and continually sharing what he learned. We should all strive to be a little more like him.

Applying
the Law of the Rubber Band
to Your Life

1. In what areas of your life have you lost your stretch and settled in? Wherever they are, you need to find internal reasons to seek the tension to stretch again. Tap into your internal discontent to get you going. Where are you falling short of your potential? What goals haven't you hit that you know you're capable of? What habits have you developed that are hindering you from moving forward? What areas of past success have you stopped winning in? Remember, change is the key to growth. Use your lack of satisfaction to get you started anyplace you've stalled.

2. Be strategic to maintain the tension between where you are and where you could be by continually resetting intermediate-range goals for yourself. If goals are too immediate, you lose the tension when you achieve them quickly. If the goals are too lofty, they can seem too difficult to achieve and become discouraging.

What is the right time frame for you to maintain the tension? Three months? Six months? A year? Set goals for yourself according to your individual personality, and then keep revisiting them at the end of those time increments. You want the goal to be just barely within reach—not too easy, but not impossible either. Being able to figure this out is an art. But it will pay tremendous dividends in your life.

3. If you need an overarching goal to keep you stretching, think about what significant action you could take if only you become what you could be. Dream big, and set this as your lifetime goal.

11

The Law of Trade-Offs

You Have to Give Up to Grow Up

*"People will cling to an unsatisfactory way of life
rather than change in order to get something better
for fear of getting something worse."*
—ERIC HOFFER

What will it take for you to go to the next level? Vision? Yes. Hard work? Of course. Personal growth? Definitely. How about letting go of some of the things that you love and value most? Yes, and believe it or not, this is the thing that often holds people back, even those who have achieved some level of success.

When you're first starting out in your career it's not very hard to give up to grow up. In fact, you're willing to give up everything for an opportunity.

Why? Because your "everything" isn't much of any-thing! But what about when you've started to earn some things: a job you enjoy, a good salary, a home, a community you've become a part of, a level of secu-rity? Are you willing to give up those things for a *chance* at doing something that will take you closer to your potential?

Achieving the American Dream

Recently I read the story of a businessman who recognized the importance of making trade-offs to become more successful and reach his potential. The son of poor service workers who worked hard and scraped for everything they had, he worked to put himself through school and earned a degree in math-ematics. He began his career working for the govern-ment, but he soon transitioned into a business career, starting with Coca-Cola, the company his father worked for as a driver. He was a manager, but he believed that his career would be limited there, since he suspected he would always be seen as the driver's son and not evaluated according to his own merits. So when he had the opportunity to take a job at Pills-bury's corporate headquarters, he took it and moved to Minnesota.

His boss at Pillsbury, whom he had gotten to know

previously at Coca-Cola, told him that they were facing a difficult challenge, and if they didn't succeed they would be looking for new jobs. That didn't intimidate him. "I have always been more motivated by the possibility of success than by the fear of failure," he explains.[1] He worked hard and set his sights on becoming a vice president by the age of forty.

At Pillsbury, he started as a manager. Soon he was promoted to group director, then senior director of management information systems, and eventually to corporate vice president of systems, where, among other things, he oversaw the construction of Pillsbury's World Headquarters, a twin-towered, forty-floor office complex in downtown Minneapolis. He completed the project ahead of schedule and under budget.

Four years before his target age, he had arrived. He was a vice president, and he had an office with a beautiful view on the thirty-sixth floor. He had achieved his dream and gone much farther than his humble beginnings might have indicated. But it wasn't enough for him. He writes,

> I was thirty-six years old and although I had been blessed to achieve so much, so fast, I knew at that moment that I had to reach for *more*. So I began to imagine how exciting it would be if I were actually the decision-maker running

a business...! After several successful years as vice president of Pillsbury's corporate systems and services, I knew that I had to dream higher; I had to dream of being *president* of something, for somebody, somewhere.[2]

If he stayed on his current track, he could never become the president of Pillsbury. His problem was that while he had always been successful and handled every responsibility with a high degree of competence, he had never been responsible for profit and loss in any position. What was he going to do? How would he achieve his dream?

From Corporate Vice President to Burger Flipper

He discussed his situation with Pillsbury's COO, and was given a possible solution. Go work for one of Pillsbury's divisions: Burger King. The move had potential, but it meant making some difficult trade-offs. He says,

My going to Burger King would mean the loss of my hard-earned, and much coveted, vice presidential title; a significant initial drop in salary; loss of stock options; the need to learn a new business from the ground up; and, if I succeeded, a potentially disruptive relocation to another part of the country."[3]

In other words, it would turn his whole life upside

You have to give up to grow up.

---

down. But that's the way the Law of Trade-Offs works. If you want to grow up to your potential, you must be willing to give up some things you value.

As he made the decision, he asked himself whether this would get him closer to his dream of being the president of a business. He also says, "I did not ask myself the wrong questions: How hard will my new job be? What will my friends think if they see me making hamburgers in a quick-service restaurant? What will I do if this new position does not work out as planned?"[4]

He made the trade-off, took the position, and dove in. He went to Burger King University, along with a bunch of recent college graduates and restaurant workers who were receiving an opportunity to become assistant managers. He was the "old dude." He learned the whole business, starting with running the broiler to making Whoppers to working the cash register and everything in between. And when his training was complete, he became a fourth assistant manager a mere fifteen-minute drive from the office where he had served as a vice president.

At Burger King, in time he moved up from assistant manager to store manager to regional manager and vice president in Philadelphia. It wasn't an easy road. He faced many challenges and there were people in the organization who didn't want to see him succeed. But he persevered, and he succeeded. "In retrospect," he says, "the unexpected obstacles I encountered at Burger King may have been a blessing in disguise. Had I anticipated them up front, I might have lost sight of my dream."[5]

Did he ever achieve that dream of becoming the president of *something*? The answer is yes. Four years after transitioning from Pillsbury's corporate offices to Burger King, he was invited to take over a failing company that Pillsbury had acquired: Godfather's Pizza. And if you haven't already guessed, the businessman's name is Herman Cain. Despite his failed bid for the presidency and the criticisms leveled at him, if you look at his life and career, you can see that he understands the Law of Trade-Offs and has often given up to grow up.

The Truth about Trade-Offs

Life has many intersections, opportunities to go up or down. At these intersections we make choices. We can add something to our life, subtract from it, or exchange something we have for something we don't. The most successful people know when to do which one of those three. Here are some insights that I hope will help you to understand trade-offs, spot them, and use them to your advantage.

Trade-Offs Are Available to Us Throughout Life

I first learned the Law of Trade-Offs when I was in elementary school, though I didn't call it that at the time. Back then, I loved to play marbles. Some days we would play marbles all during lunch and recess. It was a lot of fun trying to beat friends and win their best marbles.

A friend of mine had a big, beautiful, cat's-eye marble that I wanted very badly, but he wouldn't play with it, so I never got a chance to win it. He just held onto it and showed it to us. So I developed a strategy. I offered to trade for it. First I offered any marble I had for it. He wasn't interested. Then I offered two for it. Then three. Then four. I think he was finally willing to make the trade when I reached seven. He was happy because he had seven marbles. I was happy because I'd given up several average marbles for one beautiful one.

Everybody makes trades throughout life, whether they know it or not. The question is whether you are going to make good ones or bad ones. In general, I believe that...

Unsuccessful people make bad trade-offs.
Average people make few trade-offs.
Successful people make good trade-offs.

I estimate that I've made over twenty significant trade-offs so far during my life. I made two of them just in the last three months! At age sixty-four, I have come to realize that I have to be willing to keep making significant trade-offs if I want to keep growing and striving to reach my potential. When I stop making them, I will arrive at a dead end in life. And at that point my growth will be done. And that will be the day that my best years are behind me and my potential is no longer ahead of me.

We Must Learn to See Trade-Offs as Opportunities for Growth

Nothing creates a greater gap between successful and unsuccessful people than the choices we make. Too often, people make life more difficult for themselves because they make bad choices at the intersections of their life or they decline to make

> While we don't always get what we want, we always get what we choose.

choices because of fear. But it's important to remember that while we don't always get what we want, we always get what we choose.

Whenever I face an opportunity for a trade-off, I ask myself two questions:

WHAT ARE THE PLUSES AND MINUSES OF THIS TRADE-OFF?

Anytime you react to one of life's crossroads according to fear rather than looking at its merits, you close yourself off from a potential opportunity. By trying to figure out the pluses and minuses of any given choice, it helps me deal with that fear. Looking at cold, hard facts has also led me to discover that I have a tendency to overestimate the value of what I currently have and underestimate the value of what I may gain by giving it up.

WILL I GO THROUGH THIS CHANGE OR GROW THROUGH THIS CHANGE?

Good trade-offs are not something to be endured. That reflects a passive attitude and a mind-set that says, "I hope this turns out all right." Instead, positive trade-offs should be seen as opportunities for growth and seized. After all, we become better as a result of them. When we grow through change, we become active. We take control of our attitude and emotions. We become positive-change agents in our own lives.

Author Denis Waitley said, "A sign of wisdom and

maturity is when you come to terms with the realization that your decisions cause your rewards and consequences. You are responsible for your life, and your ultimate success depends on the choices you make." I agree with that, and years ago I determined that while others may lead timid lives, I would not. While others might see themselves as victims, I would not. While others leave their future in someone else's hands, I will not. While others simply *go* through life, I will *grow* through it. That is my choice, and I will surrender it to no one.

Trade-Offs Force Us to Make Difficult Personal Changes

Often I hear people expressing the hope that things will change. At those moments, I want to tell them that the difference between where we are and where we want to be is created by the changes we are willing to make in our lives. When you want something you have never had, you must do something you've never done to get it. Otherwise you keep getting the same results.

> The difference between where we are and where we want to be is created by the changes we are willing to make in our lives.

Changes to our lives always begin with changes we are willing to make personally. That's often not easy. But to get ourselves over the hump, we need to remember that...

Change is Personal—To change your life, *you* need to change.

Change is Possible—Everyone *can* change.

Change is Profitable—You will be rewarded when you change.

Change may not always be easy, but it can always be done. As psychologist and Holocaust survivor Viktor Frankl observed, "When we are no longer able to change a situation, we are challenged to change ourselves." We just need to remember that we are the key.

Being willing to make a change is important. So is *when* we make the change.

Changing for the sake of change gives a person whiplash.

Changing before you have to can lead to a big win, but it's difficult to do.

Changing when you have to gives you a win.

Changing after you have to leads to a loss.

Refusing to change is death to your potential.

One of the toughest personal changes I went through came in 1978. At that time, I found myself at an intersection in life. I realized that my ability to help people as a speaker was very limited. I could only touch the lives of as many people as I spoke to in person.

> "When we are no longer able to change a situation, we are challenged to change ourselves."
> —*Victor Frankl*

That's when I decided that I wanted to write books. The problem was that I had never written a book and didn't know how to do it. I realized I would have to trade much time and effort to try to become an author, but I was willing to give it a try.

I spent dozens of hours interviewing writers, taking classes, attending conferences, and listening to tapes. I spent hundreds of hours writing and revising what I'd written. The process took me a year, and all I had to show for it was a small, one-hundred-page manuscript. It was rejected by publishers, and there were several times when I asked myself, "Is all this effort really worth it?"

In the end, it did pay off. I was able to publish my first book, *Think on These Things*. Did I reach my potential writing that book? No. But it put me on the road to reaching my potential because I grew. And completing one book made it possible for me to keep writing, learning, and improving. Today, I've written more than seventy books that have sold more than 21 million copies. But I never would have sold even one book if I hadn't been willing to make the difficult changes necessary to become a writer. And I never would have reached most of the people I've had the opportunity to help.

The Loss of a Trade-Off Is Usually Felt Long Before the Gain

Not long ago I was at my son Joel's house, and I saw my grandson James, who was three, sitting in the laundry room pouting. He was waiting for his blankie to dry, and he was very unhappy because when his blanket is in the dryer, there's nothing for him to hold onto.

We are a lot like James. We want a change, but we don't want to wait for the result. And often we become acutely aware of what we have lost in the trade because we feel that immediately, while we often don't reap the benefit of the trade until days, weeks, months, years, or even decades later.

These in-between periods of transition can be a real challenge. We want the outcome, but we have to face the end of something we like and face the uncertainty between that ending and the hoped-for new beginning. The change feels like a loss. Some people deal with uncertainty fairly well; others don't. Some recover from the psychological stress of change fairly quickly and process through it successfully; others don't. How well you do will depend partly on personality and partly on attitude. You can't change your personality, but you can choose to have a positive attitude and focus on the upcoming benefits of the trade-off.

Most Trade-Offs Can Be Made at Any Time

There are many trade-offs in life that can be made at any time. For example, we can give up bad habits to acquire good ones anytime we have the willpower to make the decision. Getting an appropriate amount of sleep, trading inactivity for exercise, and developing better eating habits to improve our health are all matters of choice, not opportunity. Obviously, the sooner we make such decisions the better, but most of the time they are not time driven.

After they make a bad trade-off, people often panic, feeling that they have blown it and can never recover. But seldom is that true. Most of the time, we can make choices that will help us to come back. I know that has been true for me. I've made more than my share of poor trade-offs, but I have made many U-turns and recovered.

One of my favorite poems by Carl Bard expresses the power of making good choices after bad ones:

Though no one can go back and make
a brand new start, my friend,

Anyone can start from now
And make a brand new ending.

So when it comes to choices, never say never. Never is a long, undependable thing and life is too full of rich possibilities to have that kind of restriction placed upon it.

A Few Trade-Offs Come Only Once

The cycle of change gives us windows of opportunity in which to make decisions. Sometimes that cycle only goes around once. Miss it and the opportunity is gone. Andy Grove, former chairman and CEO of Intel, observed, "There is at least one point in the history of any company when you have to change dramatically to rise to the next performance level. Miss that moment, and you start to decline."

I experienced one of these situations a few years ago. For over a decade, the person I most wanted to meet was Nelson Mandela. It took a few years, but I was finally able to set up an appointment to spend the day with him. But as the date approached, Mr. Mandela broke his hip and he canceled the appointment. I could have changed my schedule to go meet him where he was, but it would have meant canceling a commitment I had made to speak in Kenya. That was a trade-off I was not willing to make, because I had promised to be there. Because of Mr. Mandela's age, I've probably lost the opportunity to meet with him forever.

The Higher You Climb, the Tougher the Trade-Offs

As I noted previously, if you're like most people, when you are starting out in life you have little to give up. But as you climb and accumulate some of the good things of life, the trade-offs demand a higher price. Former secretary of state Henry Kissinger said, "Each success

> "Each success only buys an admission ticket to a more difficult problem."
>
> —*Henry Kissinger*

only buys an admission ticket to a more difficult problem."

When we're at the bottom, we make trade-offs because of desperation. We are highly motivated to change. As we climb, we change because of inspiration. At this higher level we don't have to anymore. We get comfortable. As a result, we don't make the trade-offs.

One of the dangers of success is that it can make a person unteachable. Many people are tempted to use their success as permission to discontinue their growth. They become convinced that they know enough to succeed and they begin to coast. They trade innovation and growth for a formula, which they follow time after time. "You can't argue with success," they say. But they're wrong. Why? Because the skills that got you *here* are probably not the skills that will get you *there*. This is especially true today when everything is changing quickly. Five years ago (from when I am writing this), Twitter didn't exist. Now think about how it is impacting our culture and businesses. Four years ago, the iPhone didn't exist. Now it is normal to carry around this high-powered computer and communication device in a pocket. No matter how successful you have been up to this point, you can never "stand pat." If you want to keep growing and learning, you need to keep making trades. And they will cost you.

In the end, when we make trades we are trading one part of ourselves for another part. Author and thinker Henry David Thoreau said, "The price of anything is the amount of life you exchange for it." You give part of your life to receive something back. That may not be easy, but it's essential.

> "The price of anything is the amount of life you exchange for it."
> —Henry David Thoreau

Trade-Offs Never Leave Us the Same

Business book author Louis Boone asserted, "Don't fear failure so much that you refuse to try new things.

The saddest summary of life contains three descriptions: could have, might have, and should have." We all have the power of choice, but every time we make a choice, our choice has power over us. It changes us. Even the bad choices can ultimately help us to change for good, because they clarify our thinking and show us ourselves.

Professor, novelist, and apologist C. S. Lewis wrote a book called *The Great Divorce*. It's been said that he chose that title because faith requires a choice. If we truly examine it, we must decide which side of the line we want to live on, and that choice causes us to divorce ourselves from things we once held onto. So either way we choose, we aren't the same after we make the choice.

Some Trade-Offs Are Never Worth the Price

I'm all for making trade-offs. I have come to see doing them as a way of life. But not everything in my life is on the trading block. I'm not willing to trade my marriage for my career. I'm not willing to trade my relationship with my children or grandchildren for fame or fortune. And I'm not willing to trade away my values for anything or anyone. These kinds of trade-offs only lead to regret. And they are difficult to recover from.

Perhaps the most telling story of a bad trade-off

can be found in the account of Jacob and Esau in the Bible. As the older son, Esau was in line to inherit the best of everything from his father, Isaac: the birthright, the blessing, and the greater share of his father's wealth. But then he traded it all away to fill his stomach:

> One day Jacob was cooking a stew. Esau came in from the field, starved. Esau said to Jacob, "Give me some of that red stew—I'm starved!" That's how he came to be called Edom (Red).
>
> Jacob said, "Make me a trade: my stew for your rights as the firstborn."
>
> Esau said, "I'm starving! What good is a birthright if I'm dead?"
>
> Jacob said, "First, swear to me." And he did it. On oath Esau traded away his rights as the firstborn. Jacob gave him bread and the stew of lentils. He ate and drank, got up and left. That's how Esau shrugged off his rights as the firstborn.[6]

I believe that most people who make these kinds of devastating trades don't realize they're making them until after it's too late. That's why I believe it's important to create systems and draw lines to keep ourselves safe. For example, I give Margaret veto power over my schedule to keep me from spending too much time working. I also avoid being alone with any women other than family members. And I spend time every day in prayer to keep my values front and center in my life. I highly recommend that you make choices and use systems to keep yourself grounded and on track.

Trade-Offs Worth Making

What kinds of trade-offs have you been making so far in your life? Have you thought about it? Have you developed guidelines to help you decide what to strive for and what to give up in return? Allow me to give you five trade-offs that I have thought through that may help you to develop your own guidelines:

1. I Am Willing to Give Up Financial Security Today for Potential Tomorrow

Physician and writer George W. Crane said, "There is no future in any job. The future lies in the man who holds the job." I have always believed that to be true, and as a result, I have always been willing to bet on

> "There is no future in any job. The future lies in the man who holds the job."
>
> —*George W. Crane*

myself, so much so that I often accepted financial risks or pay cuts to pursue what I believed was a good opportunity.

I've made seven major career moves in my lifetime, and in five of them, I took a pay cut to do so. The first came when I chose my first job. When I graduated from college, two churches extended an invitation to me to come and lead their congregation. One offered a full-time salary. The other didn't. I chose the one that didn't pay as well because I believed I would grow more there. (And because Margaret was willing to work to help support us!) The second position I held with a larger church was an upgrade financially. That was in 1972. In all the career moves I've made since then, only one offered a financial gain—and that was in 2010!

Why was I always willing to take a pay cut when changing jobs? Because I value opportunity over security. And I knew I would work hard and be able to earn the ability to make more money in the long run.

> "The only job security we have is our individual commitment to personal development."
>
> —Kevin Turner

As my friend Kevin Turner, the COO of Microsoft, says, "The only job security we have is our individual commitment to personal development." That is a trade-off that always brings a payoff.

2. I Am Willing to Give Up Immediate Gratification for Personal Growth

I'm a very sanguine person, and I love to have fun. In fact, if you had known me when I was a boy, you probably would have predicted that my life wouldn't amount to much. I was worthless. All I ever wanted to do was play ball and spend time with my friends. But as I began to mature, I learned what opera singer Beverly Sills said: "There are no shortcuts to any-place worth going." Instant gratification and personal growth are incompatible.

My friend Darren Hardy writes in his book *The Compound Effect* about the battle most people experi-ence when it comes to weighing instant gratification against doing what's best for us:

> We understand that scarfing Pop-Tarts won't slenderize our waistlines. We realize that logging three hours a night watching *Dancing with the Stars* and *NCIS* leaves us with three fewer hours to read a good book or listen to a terrific audio. We "get" that merely purchasing great running shoes doesn't make us marathon-ready. We're a "rational" species—at least that's what we tell ourselves. So why are we so irra-tionally enslaved by so many bad habits? It's

because our need for immediate gratification can turn us into the most reactive, non-thinking animals around.[7]

When it comes to growth and success, immediate gratification is almost always the enemy of growth. We can choose to please ourselves and plateau, or we can delay our gratification and grow. It's our choice.

3. I Am Willing to Give Up the Fast Life for the Good Life

We live in a culture that idolizes movie and music stars, drools over opulent mansions, idealizes travel, and plays the lottery in hopes of someday getting the chance to live the fast life it so admires and emulates. But most of that is an illusion. It's like the airbrushed image of a model on the front of a magazine. It's not real.

That's just one of the reasons I choose to forgo the fast life in favor of the good life. What is the good life? In their book *Repacking Your Bags,* Richard J. Leider and David A. Shapiro offer a formula for the good life. They say it is "Living in the Place you belong, with the people you Love, doing the Right Work, on Purpose."[8] That's a pretty good description. I would also add what missionary Albert Schweitzer said: "The great secret of success is to go through life as a man who never gets used up." To keep myself from getting "used up," I try to create greater capacity in myself and therefore margin in my life.

If you want to create capacity and margin in your life, I suggest that you do the following:

- Delegate so you're working smarter, not just harder.
- Do what you do best and drop the rest.
- Get control of your calendar; otherwise other people will.
- Do what you love because it will give you energy.
- Work with people you like so your energy isn't depleted.

If you do those things while doing the right work with purpose in the right place with people you love, you will be living the good life.

4. I Am Willing to Give Up Security for Significance

I know many people whose goal in life is security: emotional security, physical security, and financial security. But I don't think it's wise to measure progress according to security. I think it's wiser to measure it by significance. And that requires growth. You'll never get anywhere interesting by always doing the safe thing.

> The great men and women of history were not great because of what they earned and owned, but rather for what they gave their lives to accomplish.

Most people are capable of making a living. That's the safe thing. The significant thing is making a difference. The great men and women of history were not great because of what they earned and owned, but rather for what they gave their lives to accomplish. Every trade-off is a challenge to become what we really are. Done correctly, we can create opportunities to help others become who they really are. That is significance!

5. I Am Willing to Give Up Addition for Multiplication

I started my career as an achiever. I've always had lots of energy, I get excited to do work I love, and I've never needed a lot of sleep. So I jumped into my job with both feet and I was motivated to help people. My attitude in the beginning was, "What can I do for others?" But that is addition. Once I began to learn leadership, my question changed to, "What can I do with others?" That's multiplication.

The place where I am investing the greatest amount of time, energy, and resources toward multiplication is EQUIP, the nonprofit organization I founded to teach leadership internationally. With the intention of partnering with others and helping more people, we asked ourselves,

What would happen if a leadership company would every day...

Strive to add value to leaders and organizations;
Value partnerships and aggressively pursue them;
Share, not hoard, resources and knowledge with others;
Not care who gets the credit; and
Become a river of help to others and not a reservoir of assets for themselves?

The answer is multiplication! As of today, EQUIP has trained more than 5 million leaders in 175 countries around the globe. That's something worth making trade-offs for.

If you do not already consider yourself a leader, I want to encourage you to explore developing your leadership potential. Even if you are a tiger for personal growth and greatly improve your skills and abilities, if you learn to lead, you can increase the impact you make in life. However, if you believe that you don't have it in you to lead others, then consider becoming a mentor. Your investment in others will have a multiplying effect, and you won't regret the time you give.

Most people try to take too many things with them as they journey through life. They want to keep adding without giving anything up. It doesn't work. You can't do everything; there is only so much time in a day. At some point, you reach your limit. Besides, we need to always remember that if nothing changes, nothing changes!

A lot can be learned about trade-offs from a checkers game. As someone once said: Surrender one to take two; don't make two moves at one time; move up, not down; and when you reach the top, you have the freedom to move as you like.[9] If you want to reach your potential, be ready to make trade-offs. As author James Allen said, "He who would accomplish little must sacrifice little; he who would achieve much must sacrifice much."

Applying
the Law of Trade-Offs
to Your Life

1. Write your own personal list of trade-off principles. Start by using the list in the chapter to spark ideas:

- I Am Willing to Give Up Financial Security Today for Potential Tomorrow
- I Am Willing to Give Up Immediate Gratification for Personal Growth
- I Am Willing to Give Up the Fast Life for the Good Life
- I Am Willing to Give Up Security for Significance
- I Am Willing to Give Up Addition for Multiplication

Think about worthwhile trade-offs you have made in the past that you believe will continue to be good ideas for the future. Also consider what might be needed for you to reach your potential along with what you might need to give up to fulfill it.

2. It's just as important for you to know what you *are not willing* to give up as it is to identify what you *are willing* to give up. Think through the things that are non-negotiable in your life and list them. Then for each, identify its greatest potential threat and what safety measures you need to put into place to protect it.

3. What trade do you need to make right now that you have been unwilling to make? Most people settle in and learn to live with a limitation or barrier that can be removed by making a trade. What is that next thing you need to trade for? And what must you give up to get it?

12

The Law of Curiosity

Growth Is Stimulated by Asking Why?

*"Some men see things as they are and ask why. Others
dream things that never were and ask why not."*
—George Bernard Shaw

When I was a freshman in college taking Psychology 101, everyone in the class was asked to take a creativity test. Much to my surprise and dismay, my score was among the worst in the class. *What's so bad about that?* you may ask. *Lots of people aren't very creative.* The problem was that I knew I was going to be speaking for a living, and there are few things worse than a boring speaker. How was I going to overcome this potential deficit to my career potential?

I relied on a different quality that I possessed in abundance: curiosity. I've been curious for as long as

I can remember. As a teen growing up, I was typical and very similar to my friends in most ways—except one. They loved to sleep in, but I got up early every morning. I was always afraid that if I stayed in bed, I would miss something! I find that funny now, because I lived in a little town in central Ohio where very little happened, so what was there to miss? Yet this practice set me apart from my peers.

I began to use this natural trait to collect quotes, stories, and ideas. I thought to myself, *The best way to keep from being boring is to quote people who aren't boring.* I started looking for ideas that were stated in a funny or clever or inspiring way. But guess what happened after I had done that for several years? I began to ask *why* their statements and stories were so interesting. Why were they cute? Why did people laugh at them? Why were they innovative? Why did people connect with them? Before long, I was learning from the quotes I was collecting, and I was using the same kind of slant to make my own ideas creative and memorable. It took my communication to a whole new level. And better yet, it stimulated my growth and development.

Where Does Curiosity Come From?

Was I born with this natural curiosity? Or was it something that was instilled in me? I don't know the answer, but I do know this: I have continued to be curious and to cultivate curiosity all my life. And that's important, because I believe curiosity is the key to being a lifelong learner, and if you want to keep growing and developing, you must keep on learning.

Curious people possess a thirst for knowledge. They are interested in life, people, ideas, experiences, and events, and they live in a constant state of wanting to learn more. They continually ask *why?* Curiosity is the primary catalyst for self-motivated learning. People who remain curious don't need to be encouraged to ask questions or explore. They just do it—all the time. And they keep doing it. They know that the trail to discovery is just as exciting as the discoveries themselves, because there are wonderful things to be learned along the way.

Curiosity helps a person to think and expand possibilities beyond the ordinary. Asking *why?* fires the imagination. It leads to discovery. It opens up options. It takes people beyond the ordinary and leads to extraordinary living. People say not to cross a bridge until you come to it, but as someone once said, "This world is owned by people who have crossed bridges in their imagination before anyone else has." I believe that's why Nobel Prize–winning physicist Albert Einstein said, "All meaningful and lasting change starts first in your imagination and then works its way out."

Einstein made his discoveries because he was a curious person. And he valued his curious nature and imagination as his greatest qualities.

How to Cultivate Curiosity

I love curious people. I enjoy spending time with them and conversing with them. Their excitement for knowledge and learning is contagious. I often wonder why more people aren't curious. So many people seem to be indifferent. Why don't they ask *why?* Are some people simply born without the desire to learn? Are some people just mentally lazy? Or does life become so routine for some people that they don't mind living in a rut, doing the same things day in and day out? Can such people "wake up" their minds and become more curious so growth becomes more natural to them?

I certainly hope so. I believe so. It's why I have written this chapter. And it is why I recommend the following ten suggestions for cultivating curiosity:

1. Believe You Can Be Curious

Many people fill their minds with limiting beliefs. Their lack of personal confidence or self-esteem causes them to create barriers for themselves and put limitations on how and what they think. The result?

They fail to reach their potential—not because they lack capacity but because they are unwilling to expand their beliefs and break new ground. We cannot perform outwardly in a way that is inconsistent with how we think inwardly. You cannot be what you believe you aren't. But here's the good news: You can change your thinking and as a result, your life.

Give yourself permission to be curious. The single greatest difference between curious, growing people and those who aren't is the belief that they *can* learn, grow, and change. As I explained in the Law of Intentionality, you must go after growth. Knowledge, understanding, and wisdom will not seek you out. You must go out and acquire it. The best way to do that is to remain curious.

> The single greatest difference between curious, growing people and those who aren't is the belief that they *can* learn, grow, and change.

2. Have a Beginner's Mind-Set

The way you approach life and learning has nothing to do with your age. It has everything to do with your attitude. Having a beginner's mind-set means wondering why and asking a lot of questions until you get answers. It also means being open and vulnerable. If your attitude is like that of a beginner, you have no image to uphold and your desire to learn more

> "My greatest strength as a consultant is to be ignorant and ask a few questions."
>
> —Peter Drucker

is stronger than the desire to look good. You aren't as influenced by preset rules or so-called acceptable thinking. Management expert Peter Drucker said, "My greatest strength as a consultant is to be ignorant and ask a few questions." That's having a beginner's mind-set.

People with a beginner's mind-set approach life the way that a child does: with curiosity. They are like the little girl who kept asking her mother question after question. Finally the mother cried, "For heaven's sake, stop asking so many questions. Curiosity killed the cat."

After two minutes of thinking, the child asked, "So what did the cat want to know?"

The direct opposite of people who have a beginner's mind-set are the know-it-alls. They see themselves as experts. They have a lot of knowledge, education, and experience, so instead of asking why and starting to listen, they start talking and give answers. Anytime a person is answering more than asking, you can be sure they've slowed down in their growth and have lost the fire for personal growth.

> Anytime a person is answering more than asking, you can be sure they've slowed down in their growth and have lost the fire for personal growth.

3. Make Why Your Favorite Word

Albert Einstein said, "The important thing is not to stop questioning. Curiosity has its own reason for existing. One cannot help but be in awe when he contemplates the mysteries of eternity, of life, of the marvelous structure of reality. It is enough if one tries merely to comprehend a little of this mystery every day. Never lose a holy curiosity." The secret to maintaining that "holy curiosity" is to always keep asking why.

In my early years as a leader I thought I was supposed to be an answering machine. No matter what someone asked, I gave direction, exuded confidence, and answered questions with clarity—whether I really knew what I was doing or not! As I matured, I discovered that growing leaders focused on asking questions, not giving answers. The more questions I asked, the better results we got as a team. And the greater my appetite to ask more questions. Today I have a compulsion to pick the brains of the people I meet. I have become a questioning machine.

Speaker and author Brian Tracy says, "A major stimulant to creative thinking is focused questions. There is something about a well-worded question that often penetrates to the heart of the matter and triggers new ideas and insights." Most of the time, focused questions begin with the word *why*. That word can really help you to clarify an issue. And it's important how you ask the question. People with a victim's mindset ask, "Why me?" Not because they want to know, but because they feel sorry for themselves. Curious people ask the question to find solutions so they can keep moving forward and making progress.

Scientist and philosopher Georg Christoph Lichtenberg observed, "One's first step in wisdom is to question everything—and one's last is to come to terms with everything." Those are the bookends for continuous growth. Ask why. Explore. Evaluate what you discover. Repeat. That's a pretty good formula for growth. Never forget, anyone who knows all the answers is not asking the right questions.

4. Spend Time with Other Curious People

When you think of curiosity, growth, and learning, do you think of formal education? I think in the early grades curiosity is encouraged, but after that, it's not. Most formal education steers people toward answers rather than questions. If you went to college, how many times did you hear a professor ask students to hold their questions until later so he could get through his notes or complete the syllabus? The emphasis is often on information over inquiry.

So do you find an attitude of openness and inquiry in the corporate world instead? Usually not. Most corporations don't try to stimulate curiosity either. Jerry Hirshberg, in his book *The Creative Priority: Putting Innovation to Work in Your Business*, writes,

> No one in a corporation deliberately sets out to stifle creative thought. Yet, a traditional bureaucratic structure, with its need for predictability, linear logic, conformance to accepted norms, and the dictates of the most recent "long-range" vision statement, is a nearly perfect idea-killing machine. People in groups regress toward the security of the familiar and the well-regulated. Even creative people do it. It's easier. It avoids the ambiguity, the fear of unpredictability, the threat of the unfamiliar, and the messiness of intuition and human emotion.[1]

So what must you do to cultivate curiosity and stimulate growth? You must seek out other curious people.

A couple of years ago, Margaret and I went to Jordan on vacation. We love history and art, and for years we'd heard and read about Petra, the ancient city carved out of sandstone. If you've seen *Indiana Jones and the Last Crusade*, you may remember the façade carved in stone that contained the passage to where the Holy Grail was hidden. That scene in the movie was filmed outside the Treasury in Petra.

When we visited Petra, we walked for miles. At that time, I needed knee replacement surgery, so I found the experience to be difficult and painful. By lunchtime, I was exhausted and the pain in my knee was excruciating. While we ate, the guide told us there was one more beautiful place to be seen cut in the rock. It was on the next mountain, and we could go see it, but we would have to go on our own.

Most people opted out. Like me, they were tired. I said no to the experience as well. But as we sat and ate lunch and the few who decided to make the trip prepared to leave, I started to have second thoughts. They were curious and excited about going, and their excitement started to stimulate and inspire me. My old curiosity kicked in and I couldn't stand the thought of missing something, so Margaret and I decided to join the group. It took us an hour to get up the mountain and two hours to get back down, but it was worth it. I didn't even mind having to spend most of the evening back in our hotel room soaking my knee. Being around people with great curiosity is contagious. I know of few better ways of cultivating and sustaining curiosity.

5. Learn Something New Every Day

One of the best ways to remain curious is to begin each day with a determination to learn something new, experience something different, or meet someone you don't already know. Doing this requires three things. First, you must wake up with an attitude of openness to something new. You must see the day as having multiple opportunities to learn.

Second, you must keep your eyes and ears open as you go through the day. Most unsuccessful people accept their day, tuning things out, simply hoping to endure it. Most successful people seize their day, focusing in, ignoring distractions. Growing people remain focused, yet maintain a sensitivity and awareness that opens them up to new experiences.

The third component is reflection. It does little good to see something new without taking time to think about it. It does no good to hear something new without applying it. I've found that the best way to learn something new is to take time at the end of the day to ask yourself questions that prompt you to think about what you learned. For years I've made it

> Experience is not the best teacher; evaluated experience is.

my practice to review my day and pull out the highlights. Remember, experience is not the best teacher; evaluated experience is.

6. Partake in the Fruit of Failure

A curious, growing person approaches failure in a way completely different from someone who isn't curious. Most people see failure, mistakes, and errors as signs of weakness. When they fail, they say, "I'll never do *that* again!" But people who grow and develop see failure as a sign of progress. They know that it is impossible to continually try without sometimes failing. It's part of the curiosity journey. Therefore, they make failure their friend.

When failure is your friend, you don't ask, "How can I distance myself from this experience?" Instead, you ask, "Why did this happen? What can I learn? How can I grow from this?" As a result, you fail fast, learn fast, and get to try again fast. That leads to growth and future success.

7. Stop Looking for the Right Answer

Because of my personality type, I'm someone who is always looking for options. However, I know that there are many people with different personality types who are motivated to find *the* right answer to any question. Believe it or not, that is a problem. These "single solution" people are not putting themselves in the best situation to learn and grow. Why? Because there is always more than one solution to a problem. If you believe there is only a single right solution, you either get frustrated because you can't find it, or if you think you have found it, you stop searching and perhaps miss better ideas. In addition, when you land on what you consider to be *the* right answer, you become complacent. No idea is perfect. No matter how good it is, it can always be improved.

You've probably heard the expression, "If it ain't broke, don't fix it." That phrase definitely was not coined by someone dedicated to personal growth. If that has been your mind-set in the past, then I suggest you develop a questioner's mind-set instead and replace the popular phrase with the following questions:

- If it ain't broke, how can we make it better?
- If it ain't broke, when is it likely to break in the future?
- If it ain't broke, how long will it serve as the world changes?

People with curiosity keep asking questions, and as a result, they keep learning.

Several years ago, I sold my companies so I could focus my energy and spend more time writing and speaking. But after a while, I became frustrated. I could see that the resources I had developed over many years to help others grow, develop, and learn leadership weren't reaching people the way I thought they could. So in 2011, I bought them back and started the John Maxwell Company so I could direct that process again.

I am so excited because I love my team. It's small, fast, focused, and highly talented. I've put everything in their hands and turned them loose to make things happen. And I've told them that I want them to come to work every morning convinced that there is a better way of doing everything they do, determined to find out who can help them learn to do it, and ready to make things better than they've ever been. And they're doing it!

> "Almost every advance in art, cooking, medicine, agriculture, engineering, marketing, politics, education, and design has occurred when someone challenged the rules and tried another approach."
>
> —*Roger von Oech*

Roger von Oech, author of *A Whack on the Side of the Head*, says, "Almost every advance in art, cooking, medicine, agriculture, engineering, marketing, politics, education, and design has occurred when someone challenged the rules and tried another approach."[2] If you want to avoid growing too comfortable and becoming stagnant, then keep asking questions and challenging the process. Keep asking if there is a better way to do things. Will that annoy complacent and lazy people? Yes. Will it energize, challenge, and inspire growing people? Yes!

8. Get Over Yourself

If you're going to ask questions and allow yourself to fail, then you will at times look foolish. Most people don't like that. Do you know what my response is? Get over yourself! As Roger von Oech says, "If we never tried anything that might make us look ridiculous, we'd still be in caves."

Instead, we need to be more like children. The thing I love about young children is that they just ask. They don't worry if a question is foolish. They just ask it. They don't worry about whether they will look dumb trying something new. They just do it. And as a result, they learn. Richard Thalheimer, founder of the Sharper Image, says, "It's better to look uninformed than to be uninformed. Curb your ego and keep asking questions." That's great advice.

9. Get Out of the Box

I've always loved the quote by inventor Thomas Edison, "There ain't no rules around here! We're trying to accomplish something!" Edison was forever trying to innovate, to

> **"There ain't no rules around here! We're trying to accomplish something!"**
> —*Thomas Edison*

think outside of the box. Most revolutionary ideas were disruptive violations of existing rules. They upset the old order. As Ralph Waldo Emerson said, "All life is an experiment. The more experiments you make the better."

I value innovative thinking, and I am easily frustrated by people who refuse to think outside of their self-imposed boxes. When people say things like, "We've never done it that way before" or "That's not my job," I just want to shake them up. I want to offer to do their funeral, because they've already died and are obviously just waiting for somebody to make it official. Good ideas are everywhere, but it's hard to see them when you won't look outside of your box. Instead of remaining confined, people need to break down the walls of their boxes, get out, and become hunters of ideas.

That requires an abundance mind-set. Unfortunately, most in-the-box thinkers possess a scarcity mind-set. They don't think there are many resources to go around. They believe they can't.

Author Brian Klemmer says, "One of the keys to abundance is having a solution-oriented mind-set. The average person thinks of himself as positive, but he's not solution oriented." In other words, most people live inside the box instead of outside of it. They live with their limitations. Klemmer observes,

When average people ask themselves, "Can I do this?" they base it on the circumstances they see....*An abundant thinker asks different questions.* An abundant thinker asks, *"How can I?"* This simple twist of semantics changes everything. It forces your mind to create a solution.[3]

The best way to make a sluggish mind active is to disturb its routine. Getting outside the box does that for a person.

10. Enjoy Your Life

Perhaps the greatest way to remain curious and keep growing is to enjoy life. Tom Peters, author of *In Search of Excellence*, observed, "The race will go to the curious, the slightly mad, and those with an unsatiated passion for learning and daredeviltry." I believe it honors God when we enjoy life and live it well. That means taking risks—sometimes failing, sometimes succeeding, but always learning. When you enjoy your life, the lines between work and play begin to blur. We do what we love and love what we do. Everything becomes a learning experience.

Curiosity Was His Key

Would you say that someone who earned a PhD, was a professor at a prestigious university, and won a Nobel Prize for physics had probably done a pretty good job of tapping into his potential? How about if you also learned that the person had been invited to help invent the first atomic bomb on the Manhattan Project when he was only in his twenties? That's a pretty strong résumé, isn't it? What would be the key to such a person's success? Most people would guess intelligence. But this scientist was reputed to have an above-average IQ of only 125.[4] Sure, he was intelligent, but the real secret to his growth and success was an insatiable curiosity.

His name was Richard Feynman (pronounced *Fine-man*). The son of a uniform salesman from New York City, he was always encouraged to ask questions and think for himself. As a child of eleven, he built electrical circuits and did experiments at home and soon got a reputation for being able to fix radios. He was always exploring, learning, asking why.

He began learning algebra in elementary school. He mastered trigonometry and both differential and integral calculus at age fifteen.[5] It was play for him. When his high school physics teacher became frustrated with him, he handed him a book, saying, "You talk too much and you make too much noise. I know why. You're bored. Study this book, and when you know everything that's in this book, you can talk again." It was an advanced calculus book from a course for college seniors![6] Feynman devoured it. It became another tool in his toolbox for learning about the world.

He had a lifelong love for solving puzzles and breaking codes. When he was in high school, his classmates knew this and threw at him every kind of puzzle, equation, geometry problem, or brainteaser that they could find. He solved them all.[7]

His Curiosity Knew No Bounds

Feynman's desire to know why drove him to study anything and everything. He wasn't interested only in physics or mathematics. Any idea could spark his interest. For example, when he studied physics as an undergraduate student at MIT, he took a summer job as a chemist. When he was at Princeton studying for his PhD, he would eat lunch with gradate students from other disciplines so he could learn what questions they were asking and what problems they were trying to solve. Because of that he ended up taking PhD-level courses in philosophy and biology.

That curiosity continued his entire life. One summer he decided to do advanced work in genetics.[8] Another time, on vacation in Guatemala, he taught himself how to read ancient Mayan writing, which led him to make significant mathematical and astronomical discoveries in an ancient manuscript.[9] He became an expert on art, learned to draw, and became good enough to have a one-man show.[10] He was a lifelong learner.

Feynman did experience a brief period when his curiosity waned. It was after the exhausting and demanding years he spent on the Manhattan Project. He went through a kind of slump and believed that he had burned out. He lost the will to explore. But then he figured out what the problem was. Feynman wrote,

I used to *enjoy* doing physics. Why did I enjoy it? I used to *play* with it. ... It didn't have to do with whether it was important for the development of nuclear physics, but whether it was interesting and amusing or fun to play with. When I was in high school, I'd see water running out of a faucet growing narrower, and wonder if I could figure out what determines that curve. I found it was rather easy to do. I didn't *have* to do it; it wasn't important for the future of science; somebody else had already done it. That didn't make any difference: I'd invent things and play with things for my own entertainment.

So I got this new attitude. Now that I *am* burned out, and I'll never accomplish anything...I'm going to *play* with physics, whenever I want to, without worrying about any importance whatsoever.[11]

That change in mind-set enabled him to rekindle his curiosity and cure his "burnout." As a result, he started to ask why again. Soon after this, he saw someone in the university cafeteria spin a plate by throwing it into the air. He wondered why the plate spun and wobbled the way it did. He figured it out mathematically and made some drawings, just for fun. The diagrams and math he did while doing what he called "piddling around with the wobbling plate" are what led to his receiving the Nobel Prize for Physics.[12] So he *did* end up doing things that were important to science. But that occurred simply because he wanted to know why for his own growth and satisfaction!

Feynman lived the Law of Curiosity. Do you? To know the answer, ask yourself these ten questions:

1. Do you believe you can be curious?
2. Do you have a beginner's mind-set?

3. Have you made *why* your favorite word?
4. Do you spend time with curious people?
5. Do you learn something new every day?
6. Do you partake in the fruit of failure?
7. Have you stopped looking for *the* right answer?
8. Have you gotten over yourself?
9. Do you get out of the box?
10. Are you enjoying your life?

If your answers are yes, then you probably are. If not, you need to change. And you can. Being able to answer yes to those questions has little to do with native intelligence, level of talent, or access to opportunities. It has everything to do with developing curiosity and a willingness to ask *why?*

> "The cure for boredom is curiosity. There is no cure for curiosity."
> —*Dorothy Parker*

Writer and wit Dorothy Parker observed, "The cure for boredom is curiosity. There is no cure for curiosity." How true that is. When you're curious, the entire world opens up to you and there are few limits on what you can learn and how you can develop.

Applying
the Law of Curiosity
to Your Life

1. Think about the three to five major areas in your life where you focus most of your time and energy. How do you see yourself in each of those areas? Do you think of yourself as an expert or a beginner? If you see yourself as an expert, you may be in trouble when it comes to further growth. Beginners know they have a lot to learn and are open to every possible idea. They are willing to think outside of the box. They don't get hung up on preconceived notions. They are willing to try new things.

If you have a beginner's mind-set in an area, do everything you can to maintain it. If you have come to think of yourself as an expert, beware! Find a way to rekindle a learner's attitude. Find a mentor who is ahead of you in that area. Or do what Richard Feynman did: Look for the fun again.

2. Make a list of the people you spend the most time with in a given week. Now rate each person on his or her level of curiosity. Are the majority of people

in your world questioners? Do they often ask why? Do they like to learn new things? If not, you need to make some intentional changes to spend time with more curious people.

3. One of the greatest obstacles to curiosity and learning is the reluctance to look foolish in the eyes of other people. There are two easy ways to tell if this is a potential problem in your life: The first is being afraid to fail. The second is taking yourself too seriously.

The cure is to take what I call "learning risks." Sign up to do or learn something that takes you completely out of your comfort zone. Take an art class. Sign up for dance lessons. Study a martial art. Learn a foreign language. Find a master at calligraphy or bonsai to train you. Just be certain to pick something that you find fun, where you cannot be seen as an expert, and that is far out of your comfort zone.

13

The Law of Modeling

It's Hard to Improve When You Have No One but Yourself to Follow

The most important personal-growth phrase you will ever hear a good leader say to you is "follow me."

In the Law of Intentionality chapter, I wrote about how in 1972 I searched unsuccessfully for people who had growth plans to help me learn how to develop my own. That prompted me to buy the kit that Curt Kampmeier offered and started me on the path of intentional personal growth. That provided a great start for me, but I have to admit that my early development process was hit or miss. I was learning according to trial and error.

On the positive side, personal growth became my

number one priority. I was learning how to choose books to read, lessons to listen to, and conferences to attend. At first I took a scattershot approach. I grabbed hold of anything that appealed to me. But I wasn't getting the traction I had hoped for. Then I figured out that I needed to focus my growth on my areas of personal strength: leadership, relationships, and communication. When I did that, my effectiveness in growth started to increase.

I also started to learn how to glean from what I was studying. Resources have little value unless you can pull from them the essentials that you need. That meant learning to take useful notes, gathering quotes, and reflecting on what I was learning. I often summarized what I learned and wrote action points inside the front cover of a book that was significant to me. And it meant collecting, categorizing, and filing stories and quotes every day. I also put into practice anything I learned at my earliest opportunity.

All of these practices became part of my daily discipline, and have continued to be part of it for the last forty years. My car became my classroom as I listened to tapes and later CDs. The desk in my study always had a stack of books that I was working through. My files were continually growing. I was growing, my leadership was improving, and I was seeing better results professionally.

On the negative side, I came to a realization around this same time. Personal growth without the benefit of personal mentors could take me only so far. If I wanted to become the leader I desired to be—and believed that God had created me to become—I needed to find models who were ahead of me to learn from. Why? Because it's hard to improve when you have no one but yourself to follow. That's the lesson of the Law of Modeling.

Whom Should I Follow?

I have learned a lot from people I've never met. Dale Carnegie taught me people skills when I read *How to Win Friends and Influence People* in junior high school. James Allen helped me understand that my attitude and the way that I thought would impact the course of my life when I read *As a Man Thinketh*. And Oswald Sanders revealed the importance of leadership to me for the first time when I read his book *Spiritual Leadership*. Most people who decide to grow personally find their first mentors in the pages of books. That is a great place to start. For that matter, it's a great place to continue. I am still learning from dozens

> Most people who decide to grow personally find their first mentors in the pages of books.

of people every year that I will never meet. But at some point, you must find personal models too. If you follow only yourself, you will find yourself going in circles.

I have had the privilege of connecting with many leaders whose modeling I have found worthy of imitation. People such as consultant Fred Smith, speaker Zig Ziglar, and coach John Wooden have helped me tremendously. Others, who looked better from a distance than they actually were when I got to know them, turned out to be disappointments. Which just goes to show that you must be selective when it comes to choosing mentors and models.

I smile every time I think of the two derelicts sunning themselves on a park bench. The first guy said, "The reason I'm here is because I refused to listen to anyone."

The second guy responded, "The reason I'm here is because I listened to everyone."

Neither course of action is helpful. You must be selective in who you choose as a mentor. From both the positive and the negative experiences I've had with mentors, I have developed criteria to determine the "worthiness" of a model for me to follow. I share them with you in the hope that they will help you to make good choices for this area of your growth.

1. A Good Mentor Is a Worthy Example

We become like the people we admire and the models we follow. For that reason, we should take great care when determining which people we ask to mentor us. They must not only display professional excellence and possess skill sets from which we can learn, they must also demonstrate character worthy of emulating.

Many athletes, celebrities, politicians, and business leaders today try to disavow being any kind of role model when others are already following them and mimicking their behavior. They want people to separate their personal behavior from their professional life, but such a division cannot really be made. Religious leader and author Gordon B. Hinckley advised,

> It is not wise, or even possible, to divorce private behavior from public leadership—though there are those who have gone to great lengths to suggest that this is the only possible view of "enlightened" individuals. They are wrong. They are deceived. By its very nature, true leadership carries with it the burden of being an example. Is it asking too much of *any* public officer, elected by his or her constituents, to stand tall and be a model before the people—not only in the ordinary aspects of leadership

but in his or her behavior? If values aren't established and adhered to at the top, behavior down the ranks is seriously jeopardized and undermined. Indeed, in any organization where such is the case—be it a family, a corporation, a society, or a nation—the values being neglected will in time disappear.

As you look for role models and mentors, scrutinize their personal lives as carefully as their public performance. Your values will be influenced by theirs, so you shouldn't be too casual who you choose to follow.

2. A Good Mentor Is Available

Steel magnate and philanthropist Andrew Carnegie said, "As I grow older I pay less attention to what men say. I just watch what they do." For us to be able to observe models up close and see what they do, we must have some contact with them. That requires access and availability. For us to be actively mentored, we must have time with people to ask questions and learn from their answers.

> "As I grow older I pay less attention to what men say. I just watch what they do."
> —Andrew Carnegie

When I mentor people, we usually meet officially only a few times a year. However, during the year we sometimes spend time together informally. Many of their mentoring questions are stimulated by my actions, not my words. That thought humbles me, because I know at times I fall short of the ideals and values that I teach. As I have often said, my greatest leadership challenge is leading me! Teaching people what to do is easy. Showing them is much more difficult.

> My greatest leadership challenge is leading me!

The greatest piece of advice I can give in the area of availability is that when you are looking for a mentor, don't shoot too high too soon. If you're considering going into politics for the first time, you don't need the advice of the president of the United States. If you are a high school student thinking about learning to play the cello, you don't need to be mentored by Yo-Yo Ma. If you're fresh out of school and just starting your career, don't expect to get extensive mentoring time from the CEO of your organization.

Why shouldn't I? you may be thinking. *Why not start with the best?* First of all, if you're just starting out, nearly all of your questions can be answered by someone two or three levels ahead you of you (not ten). And their answers will be fresh because they will have recently dealt with the issues you're dealing with.

Second, CEOs need to be spending their time answering the questions of the people who are on the verge of leading at their level. I'm not saying you should never go to the top. I'm saying spend the majority of your time being mentored by people who are available, willing, and suited for the stage of your career. And as you progress in your development, find new mentors for your new level of growth.

3. A Good Mentor Has Proven Experience

The farther you go in the pursuit of your potential, the more new ground you will have to break. How do you figure out how to proceed? Benefit from others' experience. As the Chinese proverb says, "To know the road ahead, ask those coming back."

> "To know the road ahead, ask those coming back."
> —Chinese proverb

In the early 1970s when my church was growing rapidly, I realized I was moving into territory that I hadn't been in before, nor had anyone I knew. To help me figure out how to lead better in this new territory, I began to seek out successful church leaders in larger churches around the country. I've told the story many times of how I offered $100 to them for thirty minutes of their time. Many graciously agreed to meet with me. I'd go to the meeting armed with a legal pad full of questions and pick their brains. I can hardly explain how much I learned in those sessions.

Every time I've entered into a new venture, I've sought the advice of people with proven experience. When I started my first business, I talked to successful businesspeople who could give me advice. When I wanted to write my first book, I sat at the feet of successful authors who could guide me. To learn to communicate more effectively, I studied communicators. Hearing about their bad experiences made me aware of potential problems I would be facing up the road. Hearing about their good experiences gave me an anticipation of potential opportunities up ahead of me.

I don't know of a successful person who hasn't learned from more experienced people. Sometimes they follow in their footsteps. Other times they use their advice to help them break new ground. Former New York City mayor Rudy Giuliani says, "All leaders are influenced by those they admire. Reading about them and studying their traits inevitably allows an inspiring leader to develop his own leadership traits."

> "All leaders are influenced by those they admire. Reading about them and studying their traits inevitably allows an inspiring leader to develop his own leadership traits."
>
> —*Rudy Giuliani*

4. A Good Mentor Possesses Wisdom

There's a well-known story of an expert who was called by a company to look at their manufacturing system. It had broken and everything was at a standstill. When the expert arrived, he carried nothing but a little black bag.

Silently he walked around the equipment for a few minutes and then stopped. As he focused on one specific area of the equipment, he pulled a small hammer out of his bag and he tapped it gently. Suddenly everything began running again, and he quietly left.

The next day he sent a bill that made the manager go ballistic. It was for $1,000! Quickly the manager e-mailed the expert and wrote, "I will not pay this outrageous bill without it being itemized and explained." Soon he received an invoice with the following words:

For the tapping on equipment with hammer—$1.

For knowing where to tap—$999.

That is the value of wisdom! Mentors with wisdom often show us where to tap. Their understanding, experience, and knowledge help us to solve problems that we would have a hard time handling on our own.

Fred Smith was a mentor who often deposited wisdom into my life. One day I asked him why highly successful people often sabotaged their lives and hurt their careers. He said, "Never confuse the giftedness of a person with the person. Their gifts allow them to do amazing things but the person may be flawed, which will eventually cause harm." That bit of wisdom has helped me immeasurably. First, it has helped me to better understand how to work with talented people and to help them develop. Second, it has been a caution to me personally. I know that having talent in a given area never exempts me from neglecting discipline or character issues. We're all just one step away from stupid.

Wise people often use just a few words to help us learn and develop. They open our eyes to worlds we might not have otherwise seen without their help. They help us navigate difficult situations. They help us to see opportunities we would otherwise miss. They make us wiser than our years and experience.

5. A Good Mentor Provides Friendship and Support

The first question most followers ask of a mentor is, "Do you care for me?" The reason for this question

"Great things happen whenever we stop seeing ourselves as God's gift to others, and begin seeing others as God's gift to us."
—*James S. Vuocolo*

is obvious. Who wants to be guided by a person who isn't interested in them? Selfish people will assist you only insofar as it advances their own agenda. Good mentors provide friendship and support, unselfishly working to help you reach your potential. Their mind-set is well expressed by business coach and author James S. Vuocolo, who says, "Great things happen whenever we stop seeing ourselves as God's gift to others, and begin seeing others as God's gift to us."

One evening I was enjoying dinner with the former CEO of Girl Scouts Frances Hesselbein and author Jim Collins. Both were mentored by Peter Drucker, often called the father of modern management. I had met Drucker and learned from him, but they had enjoyed a long-term relationship with him and had known him well. I asked them what they had learned from him, and their responses focused on the friendship of the man more than the wisdom of the expert. What Jim Collins told me that night is expressed very succinctly in an article he wrote after Drucker's death:

But for me, Drucker's most important lessons cannot be found in any text or lecture but in the example of his life. I made a personal pilgrimage to Claremont, California, in 1994 seeking wisdom from the greatest management thinker of our age, and I came away feeling that I had meet a compassionate and generous human being who—almost as a side benefit— was a prolific genius. We have lost not a guru on a pedestal but a beloved professor who welcomed students into his modest home for warm and stimulating conversation. Peter F. Drucker was driven not by the desire to say something but the desire to learn something from every student he met—and that is why he became one of the most influential teachers most of us have ever known.[1]

If the person who offers to mentor you doesn't really support you and offer you friendship, then the relationship will always fall short of your expectations. Knowledge without support is sterile. Advice without friendship feels cold. Candor without care is harsh. However, when you are being helped by someone who cares for you it is emotionally satisfying. Growth comes from both the head and the heart. Only supportive people are willing to share both with you.

6. A Good Mentor Is a Coach Who Makes a Difference in People's Lives

A major theme in my life is the desire to add value to people and make a difference in their lives. One of the ways I do that is by mentoring people. But my time is so limited that I can mentor only a very few. This has caused frustration for me and for the many people who ask me to coach them or train them to coach others. To my delight, I finally have a solution to this problem.

In 2011, some friends helped me to create a coaching company called the John Maxwell Team. It has become one of my most fulfilling "make a difference" commitments because it enables me to add value to many people by helping to train and certify coaches who teach my principles. Together, we are making a difference in people's lives.

I love the word *coach*. I read in my friend Kevin Hall's book *Aspire* that the word derives from the horse-drawn coaches that were developed in the town of Kocs during the fifteenth century. The vehicles were originally used to transport royalty, but in time they also carried valuables, mail, and common passengers. As Kevin remarks, "A 'coach' remains something, or someone, who *carries a valued person from where they are to where they want to be.*" So if you had a coach, you knew you would end up at your desired destination. In a piece called, "A Coach By Any Other Name," Kevin goes on to describe what it means to be a coach. He writes,

> In other cultures and languages, coaches are known by many different names and titles.
>
> In Japan, a "sensei" is one who has gone farther down the path. In martial arts, it is the designation for master.
>
> In Sanskrit, a "guru" is one with great knowledge and wisdom. "Gu" means darkness, and "ru" means light—a guru takes someone from darkness into the light.
>
> In Tibet, a "lama" is one with spirituality and authority to teach. In Tibetan Buddhism, the Dalai Lama is the highest-ranking teacher.
>
> In Italy, a "maestro" is a master teacher of music. It is short for "maestro de cappella," meaning master of the chapel.
>
> In France, a "tutor" is a private teacher. The term dates to the fourteenth century and refers to one who served as a watchman.
>
> In England, a "guide" is one who knows and shows the way. It denotes the ability to see and point out the better course.

> "A 'coach' remains something, or someone, who *carries a valued person from where they are to where t hey want to be.*
>
> —*Kevin Hall*

In Greece, a "mentor" is a wise and trusted advisor. In *The Odyssey*, Homer's Mentor was a protective and supportive counselor.

All these words describe the same role: *one who goes before and shows the way.*[2]

No matter what word you use to describe them, coaches make a difference in others' lives. They help them grow. They improve their potential. They increase their productivity. They are essential to helping people effect positive change. As my friend Andy Stanley says in *The Next Generation Leader,* "You will never maximize your potential in any area without coaching. It is impossible. You may be good. You may be even better than everyone else. But without outside input you will never be as good as you could be. We all do better when somebody is watching and evaluating....Self-evaluation is helpful, but evaluation from someone else is essential."[3]

> "Self-evaluation is helpful, but evaluation from someone else is essential."
>
> —*Andy Stanley*

In my opinion, good coaches share five common characteristics. They...

- **C**are for the People they Coach
- **O**bserve their Attitudes, Behavior, and Performance
- **A**lign Them with Their Strengths for Peak Performance
- **C**ommunicate and Give Feedback about Their Performance
- **H**elp Them to Improve Their Lives and Performance

I have benefitted from hundreds of people over the years who have modeled personal growth, mentored me from their successes, and coached me to better performance by using these five characteristics. I am indebted to them.

The process of growing with the help of a mentor usually follows this pattern: It begins with awareness. You realize that you need help and that following yourself is not a viable option for effective personal growth. I was fortunate to come to this realization early in my career. I recognized that I had no experience, no exposure, and no strong models within my circles to help me develop my potential.

When a person comes to such a realization, one of two things can happen. The first is that the person's pride swells up and he cannot bring himself to ask another person for advice. This is a common reaction.

In his book *The Corporate Steeplechase*, psychologist Srully Blotnick says that people in their twenties starting their careers tend to be ashamed to ask questions. When they reach their thirties their desire to be individualistic makes it difficult for them to seek counsel from colleagues. That can definitely work against them. To keep from looking ignorant, they almost ensure their own ignorance.

The other reaction to awareness is to humble yourself and say, "I need your help." That decision not only leads to greater knowledge, but it also often develops maturity. It reinforces that people need one another—not just when they're young and starting out, but their entire lives. As Chuck Swindoll so eloquently says in his book *The Finishing Touch*,

> Nobody is a whole chain. Each one is a link. But take away one link and the chain is broken.
>
> Nobody is a whole team. Each one is a player. But take away one player and the game is forfeited.
>
> Nobody is a whole orchestra. Each one is a musician. But take away one musician and the symphony is incomplete...
>
> You guessed it. We need each other. You need someone and someone needs you. Isolated islands we're not.

To make this thing called life work, we gotta lean and support. And relate and respond. And give and take. And confess and forgive. And reach out and embrace. And release and rely....

Since none of us is a whole, independent, self-sufficient, super-capable, all-powerful hotshot, let's quit acting like we are. Life's lonely enough without our playing that silly role.

The game's over. Let's link up.

As I look back over my life, I recognize that the greatest assets of my growth journey were people. But then again, so were the greatest liabilities. The people you follow, the models you emulate, the mentors you take advice from help to shape you. If you spend your time with people who subtract from you, who belittle you or undervalue you, then every step forward that you attempt to take will be difficult. But if you find wise leaders, good role models, and positive friends, you will find that they speed you on your journey.

I've been fortunate to have many fantastic mentors during the course of my life. My first models were my parents, Melvin and Laura Maxwell. From them I learned integrity and unconditional love. Elmer Towns and Zig Ziglar were two of the people I first learned from outside of the small circle I grew up in. Elmer was the first to teach me about growing my church. Zig was the first personal-growth speaker I followed. Both became good friends. Tom Philippe and my brother Larry Maxwell mentored me in business. Les Stobbe helped me learn how to write my first book. Peter Drucker opened my eyes to the importance of developing people to the level where they could replace me. Fred Smith helped me to fine-tune my leadership skills. Bill Bright showed me the impact that business thinkers can have on the world of faith. John Wooden taught me how to be a better man.

No matter who you are, what you have accomplished, how low or how high your life has taken you, you can benefit from having a mentor. If you've never had one, you have no idea how much it can improve your life. If you have had mentors, then you already know—and you should start passing it on by becoming a mentor to others, because you know that it's hard to improve when you have no one but yourself to follow.

Applying
the Law of Modeling
to Your Life

1. Find a next-step mentor. Think about where you are currently in your career and the direction you would like to go. Look for someone you admire who is two or three steps ahead of you on that same track. This person doesn't necessarily need to be in your organization. Look for the qualities needed in a good mentor: a worthy example, availability, proven experience, wisdom, willingness to be supportive, and coaching skills. If those are present in this individual, ask him or her to mentor you.

Before any meeting with a mentor, come prepared with three to five thoughtful questions, the answers to which will help you significantly. After you've met, work to apply what you've learned to your own situation. Don't ask for another meeting until you have done that. At your next meeting, begin the session by telling your mentor how you applied what you learned (or how you tried to apply it and failed so you can learn what you did wrong). Then ask your new questions. Follow this pattern, and your mentor will be rewarded for his or her effort and will probably be glad to continue helping you.

2. We all need people who can help us sharpen specific strengths or navigate through certain problem areas. Who do you talk to when you have questions related to marriage, parenting, spiritual growth, personal disciplines, hobbies, and so on? No one person can answer all of these questions. You need to find several individual "consultants" to help you.

Spend some time making two lists. First, list the specific strengths or skills you want to improve to reach your potential. Second, list the specific problem areas where you feel the need for ongoing guidance. Begin looking for people with expertise in these particular areas and ask them if they would be willing to answer questions when you have them.

3. Do you have long-term models whom you observe, follow, and learn from, people who can give you advice regarding the big picture of your life and career? Or are you trying to improve while having no one but yourself to follow? If you haven't been asking others to help you on your journey, it's time to start. Most of us begin by looking for worthy models to follow by reading about them in books. Start there. But

don't leave it at that. Look for people who will give you access to their lives.

One such person for me was John Wooden. For many decades, I learned from him from a distance. I watched his teams play on television. I followed his career. I read everything he wrote. However, when he was in his nineties, I had the privilege of meeting with him twice a year for several years. I learned a lot from him and I'm very grateful for the time I had with him.

As you look for models and mentors, I want to give you a word of caution. Oftentimes, people look good from far away, but when you get to know them, you discover qualities you don't admire. If that happens to you, please don't allow it to discourage you. There are plenty of people out there who have integrity and who are worthy to be respected and followed (such as John Wooden). Keep looking for them and you will find them.

14

The Law of Expansion

Growth Always Increases Your Capacity

"There is no finish line."
—Nike commercial

Have you maxed out your capacity? Have you reached your full potential as a person? I believe that if you are reading this, the answer is no. If you're still breathing and you are of sound mind, then you have the potential to keep increasing your capacity. In their book *If It Ain't Broke... Break It!* authors Robert J. Kriegel and Louis Patler write,

> We don't have a clue as to what people's limits are. All the tests, stopwatches, and finish lines in the world can't measure human potential. When someone is pursuing their dream, they'll

go far beyond what seems to be their limitations. The potential that exists within us is limitless and largely untapped...when you think of limits, you create them.[1]

> "The potential that exists within us is limitless and largely untapped...when you think of limits, you create them."
>
> —*Robert J. Kriegel and Louis Patler*

How do you push toward your potential and keep increasing your capacity? I've written quite a bit about how to increase your effectiveness *externally*. You do that by including others and learning how to work with people. But the only way to increase your capacity *internally* is to change the way you approach personal growth. Learning more information isn't enough. You must change how you think and you must change your actions.

How to Increase Your Thinking Capacity

I've heard that most experts believe people typically use only 10 percent of their true potential. That statement is staggering! If that is true, then the average person has huge capacity for improvement. It's as if we possess hundreds of acres of possibilities but keep only half an acre under cultivation. So how do we tap into the unused 90 percent? The answer is

> Most experts believe people typically use only 10 percent of their true potential.

found in changing how we think and what we do. Let's start by looking at how you need to think to increase your capacity.

1. Stop Thinking More Work and Start Thinking What Works?

Ask most people how they can increase their capacity and they'll tell you by working more. There's a problem with that solution. More work will not necessarily increase your capacity. More of the same usually results in more of the same, when what we actually want is better than what we have.

I fell into this trap early in my career. In fact, when people began asking me to help them be more successful, my answer to them was to work harder. I assumed that their work ethic wasn't as good as mine, and if they would simply do more, they would be successful. However, I realized the error in my thinking when I started traveling to undeveloped countries where many people worked very hard but saw very little return for all their efforts. I learned that hard work isn't always the answer.

That prompted me to start looking at the way I approached my working life. Being a high-energy person, I worked hard and kept it up for long hours. But I knew that I wasn't as effective as I could be.

I realized that the problem was that I valued effort over effectiveness. I was doing a lot of things instead of the right things. My to-do list kept getting longer, but my impact wasn't increasing. I realized that I had to change my thinking. I looked at everything I was doing and started to ask myself, "What works?"

That's what I recommend you do. Figure out what works. To do that, ask yourself the following three questions:

What am I required to do?
What gives the greatest return?
What gives me the greatest reward?

These questions will help you to focus your attention on what you must do, what you ought to do, and what you really want to do.

2. Stop Thinking Can I? and Start Thinking How Can I?

At first glance, the questions *Can I?* and *How can I?* may appear to be very similar. However, the reality is that they are worlds apart in terms of results. *Can I?* is a question filled with hesitation and doubt. It is a question that imposes limitations. If that is the question you regularly ask yourself, you're undermining your efforts before you even begin. How many people could have accomplished much in life but failed to try because they doubted and answered no to the question "Can I?"

When you ask yourself "How can I?" you give yourself a fighting chance to achieve something. The most common reason people don't overcome the odds is that they don't challenge them enough. They don't test their limits. They don't push their capacity. *How can I?* assumes there is a way. You just need to find it.

> The most common reason people don't overcome the odds is that they don't challenge them enough.

As a young leader, I was challenged by the words of Robert Schuller, who said, "What would you attempt if you knew you couldn't fail?" To me the answer was obvious. A lot more than I was currently attempting! Schuller's question prompted me to think outside the box. It made me want to take more risks, to push more boundaries, to test my own limits. It made me realize that most of our limitations are based not on lack of ability, but lack of belief.

Sharon Wood, the first North American woman to climb Mount Everest, said of her experience, "I discovered it wasn't a matter of physical strength, but a matter of psychological strength. The conquest lay within my own mind to penetrate those barriers of

self-imposed limitations and get to the good stuff—
the stuff called potential, 90 percent of which we
barely use." If you want to tap into that unused 90 percent, ask "How can I?" Do that and greater achievement becomes a matter of when and how, not if.

Recently a friend gave me a book by Price Pritchett entitled, *You²*. In it Pritchett writes,

> Your skepticism, which you presume is based
> on rational thinking and an objective assess-
> ment of factual data about yourself, is rooted in
> mental junk. Your doubts are not the product of
> accurate thinking, but habitual thinking. Years
> ago you accepted flawed conclusions as correct,
> began to live your life as if those warped ideas
> about your potential were true, and ceased the
> bold experiment in living that brought you
> many breakthrough behaviors as a child. Now
> it's time for you to find that faith you had in
> yourself before.[2]

If you have spent time in a negative environment
or you have experienced abuse in your life, you may
find this thinking transition to be very difficult. If
that describes you, then let me take a moment to
encourage you and explain something. I'm asking you
to shift from *Can I?* to *How can I?* when maybe you

need to change your thinking from *I can't!* to *How can I?* I believe that if you've gotten this far in this book, then deep down you already believe that you can achieve things. I believe you can too. I believe God has put in *every* person the potential to grow, expand, and achieve. The first step in doing that is believing that you can. I believe in you!

The second is perseverance. As you get started, it may not look like you're making progress. That doesn't matter. Don't give up. Pritchett says that everything looks like a failure in the middle. He writes, "You can't bake a cake without getting the kitchen messy. Halfway through surgery it looks like there's been a murder in the operating room. If you send a rocket to the moon, about ninety percent of the time it's off course—it 'fails' its way to the moon by continually making mistakes and correcting them."[3]

> Everything looks like a failure in the middle.

You can change your thinking. You can believe in your potential. You can use failure as a resource to help you find the edge of your capacities. As psychiatrist Fritz Perls observed, "Learning is discovering that some-

> "Learning is discovering that something is possible."
> —*Fritz Perls*

thing is possible." The Law of Expansion is about learning, growing, increasing our capacity.

It's said that one day the great artist Michelangelo went into the studio of Raphael. He looked at one of his early drawings, considered it a moment, then took a piece of chalk and wrote the word *Amplius*, which means "greater" or "larger," across the entire drawing. Michelangelo was encouraging Raphael to think bigger. That's what we need to do.

3. Stop Thinking One Door and Start Thinking Many Doors

When it comes to growth, you don't want to stake your future on one "door." It may not open! It's much better to consider many possibilities and look for multiple answers to all of your questions. Think in terms of options.

I made the mistake of looking for the one door early in my career. I wanted to build a great church, so I went looking for the key that would lead me to success. I started interviewing people to find someone who could give me "the secret." It was almost like I was looking for someone who could grant my wish. My thinking was all wrong. I wanted someone to give me a formula for my dream so I could act on it. In time I came to realize that I needed to act on my dream and formulate the details as I made the journey. Mobility was critical to progress, and my strategy began to evolve out of my discovery process.

One of my favorite words is *options*. Anyone who knows me well understands that I don't like being "fenced in." But my desire for options is driven by more than just the desire to avoid mental claustrophobia. It's driven by the desire to increase my capacity. The more time goes by, the more I want to explore creative options and the less I want to rely on someone else's system.

As I have learned to think *many doors* and explore options, here is what I have learned:

- There is more than one way to do something successfully.
- The odds of arriving anywhere increase with creativity and adaptability.
- Movement with intentionality creates possibilities.
- Failures and setbacks can be great tools for learning.
- Knowing the future is difficult; controlling the future is impossible.
- Knowing today is essential; controlling today is possible.

Knowing the future is difficult; controlling the future is impossible. Knowing today is essential; controlling today is possible.

- Success is a result of continued action filled with continual adjustments.

The greatest challenge you will ever face is that of expanding your mind. It's like crossing the great frontier. You must be willing to be a pioneer, to enter uncharted territory, to face the unknown, to conquer your own doubts and fears. But here's the good news. If you can change your thinking, you can change your life. As Oliver Wendell Holmes remarked, "Man's mind, once stretched by a new idea, never regains its original dimensions." If you want to expand your capacity, the first place to start is always in your own mind.

> "Man's mind, once stretched by a new idea, never regains its original dimensions."
> —*Oliver Wendell Holmes*

How to Increase Your Capacity for Action

If you want to expand your potential and therefore your capacity, you must first change your thinking. However, if you change *only* your thinking and you neglect to change your actions, you will fall far short of your potential. To start expanding your capacity, take the following three steps:

1. Stop Doing Only Those Things You Have Done Before and Start Doing Those Things You Could and Should Do

The first step toward success is becoming good at what you know how to do. But the more that you do what you know, the more you discover additional worthy things you *could* do. When this occurs, you have a decision to make. Will you continue doing what you have always done, or will you make the leap and try new things? Doing new things leads to innovation and new discoveries, and among those discoveries is the realization of things you *should* do on a consistent basis. If you do those, you will continue to grow and expand your potential. If you don't, you will plateau.

My friend Kevin Hall describes this process of discovery and growth in *Aspire* when he writes about a discussion he had with one of his mentors, retired professor Arthur Watkins. The gentleman was describing the growth of a tradesman from apprentice to master. Kevin recalls their conversation:

A master didn't become a master overnight, he explained. There was a process. First, one must become an apprentice, then a journeyman, and finally a master.

Apprentice. Journeyman. Master. These three words illustrate the importance of going through fundamental and necessary steps to acquire the kind of humility that is commensurate with true leadership.

Arthur grew quite animated as if he were about to reveal an ancient truth. "Do you know that 'apprentice' means *learner*?" he asked, then taught that the word comes from the French "appendre," which means *to learn*.

In earlier times, apprentice was the name for someone who would select a trade, then find a master in his village to teach him the skills necessary for his chosen vocation. After learning all he could from the local master, the apprentice would then travel elsewhere to broaden his education. Launching forward on such a journey turned an apprentice into a journeyman. A journeyman would often travel long distances for the privilege of working under the master who could best help him further hone his craft. Over time, a journeyman could eventually become a master himself—and be in a position to start the cycle all over again.[4]

The process of expanding one's potential is ongoing. It ebbs and flows. Opportunities come and go.

The standards we must set for ourselves are constantly changing. What we *could* do changes as we develop. What we *should* do also evolves. We must leave behind some old things to take on new ones. It can be difficult work, but if we are willing, our lives are changed.

In 1974 I became convinced that everything rises and falls on leadership. With that conviction came a passion for leading. I was fired up to learn how to lead effectively and then touch others. After several years I achieved a level of comfort in my ability to lead others and teach on the subject. I was enjoying what I did and seeing a degree of success. But then I began to see opportunities, other things I *could* do. I had the chance to reach a larger audience. I was at a decision point. Should I enjoy my life or attempt to expand it?

Expansion would mean leaving my comfort zone. I would have to start a business to produce teaching materials. I would have to develop people who could work alongside me. I would have to learn to write books so I could reach people I'd never get to speak to. I would need to travel and learn the customs and cultures of those who lived in other countries to be able to

> **"I am always doing that which I cannot do, in order to learn how to do it."**
> —*Pablo Picasso*

communicate outside of the United States. All these changes took time. I made a lot of mistakes. Often I was in over my head. Most days I felt like Pablo Picasso when he said, "I am always doing that which I cannot do, in order to learn how to do it."

The process of adaptation and expansion has continued for me and still does. More recently, I've had to learn how to use social media to expand my reach. I've started two companies. I've learned how to start a coaching initiative. And I'm continuing to learn how to connect with people in other countries around the globe. I never want to stop learning. I want to keep enlarging myself, expanding my potential, and improving my craft to my dying day. I want to live out the words of author and pastor Norman Vincent Peale, who said, "Ask the God who made you to keep remaking you."

2. Stop Doing What Is Expected and Start Doing More Than Is Expected

We live in a culture that awards trophies to people for simply showing up, regardless of their contribution. Because of that, many people think they are doing well if they just do what is expected of them. I don't

> We live in a culture that awards trophies to people for simply showing up, regardless of their contribution.

believe that helps people reach their potential or expand their capacity. To do that, a person has to do more.

Former General Electric CEO Jack Welch calls this "getting out of the pile." To distinguish yourself, get noticed, and advance your career, you need to do and be more. You have to rise above average. You can do this by asking more of yourself than others ask, expecting more from yourself than others expect, believing more in yourself than others believe, doing more than others think you should have to do, giving more than others think you should give, and helping more than others think you should help.

I like the way boxer Jack Johnson described it: "Going *far* beyond that call of duty, doing *more* than others expect, this is what excellence is all about! And it comes from *striving*, maintaining the *highest* standards, looking after the *smallest* detail, and going the *extra* mile. Excellence means doing your *very* best. In *everything!* In *every* way."

Doing more than is expected does more than just separate you from your colleagues by earning you a reputation for performance. It also trains you to develop a habit for excellence. And that compounds over time. Continued excellence expands your capabilities and your potential.

3. Stop Doing Important Things Occasionally and Start Doing Important Things Daily

Have you ever heard the expression "Life is a great big canvas and you should throw all the paint on it that you can"? I like the intent and exuberance of those words, but I don't think that advice is very good—unless you want a mess. A better thought is to make your life a masterpiece, which requires much thought, a clear idea, and selection when it comes to what paint you put on the canvas. How do you do that? By doing the important things every day.

Writer and philosopher Henry David Thoreau wrote,

> If one advances confidently in the direction of his dreams, and endeavors to live the life which he has imagined, he will meet with a success unexpected in common hours. He will pass an invisible boundary; new, universal, and more liberal laws will begin to establish themselves around and within him; and he will live with the license of a higher order of beings.

I believe advancing confidently in the direction of one's dreams means doing what is important every day. To do what's not important every day does nothing for you. It merely uses up your time. To do the right thing only occasionally does not lead to consistent growth and the expansion of your life. Both components are necessary. Daily growth leads to personal expansion.

Poet Henry Wadsworth Longfellow compared his growth to that of an apple tree. He said, "The purpose of that apple tree is to grow a little new wood each year. That is what I plan to do." He also expressed a similar thought in one of his poems when he wrote,

> *Not enjoyment and not sorrow is our destined end*
> *   always;*
> *But to live that each tomorrow finds us further than*
> *   today.*

If we do what's important every day, that can be true for us.

Expanding His Capacity—and His Impact

One of the greatest rewards I receive from writing and speaking is occasionally hearing from someone who has been positively impacted by my work. Recently I received a letter from Tim Williams, a sergeant who works for the county sheriff's office in Colorado Springs, Colorado. He wrote to tell me about the intentional-growth path he has been taking and how it has expanded his capacity. Tim wrote,

As a part of my promotional testing process in 2005, I was required to read *The 21 Irrefutable Laws of Leadership.* I had told myself that I would first read each of the books I was assigned, then re-read each, and finally skim each with a highlighter to obtain possible test questions. My first read of *The 21 Laws* did not leave me with a favorable opinion. My re-read left me feeling better and agreeing with most of it. As I skimmed it I came to the conclusion that I had been under a leadership rock for the better part of my life. Prior to being a sergeant with the sheriff's office I had spent twenty years as a sergeant in the U.S. Army Special Forces, [so] I didn't consider leadership a new concept.

Tim went on to say that he continues to read books as part of his growth plan. They have changed his thinking—and his actions. As a result, he has continued to advance within the organization. "As I was promoted in rank," he wrote, "I have also been able to institute several changes within my organization that

I credit directly to what I have learned.... I have been able to influence others and help many."

Tim has adopted two practices as a result of what he's learned. The first is that he goes to where his employees are. Tim said, "I spent my nights in the jail going from station to station visiting with deputies and just talking about anything. I listened, laughed, and just spent time hearing about their families and on some occasions their complaints." As a result, he started connecting with people. The second was writing personal notes to people to let them know that he cares about them and appreciates their work. He also became very intentional about noting in their evaluations the positive things his employees did, not just their deficiencies. "The increase in morale was amazing," said Tim.

Tim went on to say, "At year's end I decided to take this one step further and send an e-mail to all those assigned to my shift. I wanted it to be positive and transparent to all. I have made this an annual event and the results have been fantastic! My shift sick-time usage dropped markedly. I've enclosed the first edition of what I call 'Thanks, I Noticed'":

Shift 4,
As we come to the end of the year, I wanted to take a moment and reflect on the things that all of you have

done individually to make my life easier as a supervisor. Because of the competitive nature of this profession we share, I want all of you to collectively know what you have done for each other. As this year has passed, in some way each of you has contributed to the success that we all share.

So for all the little things that you may have thought went unnoticed, please let me say, Thank you, I noticed.

Michael B., for giving up your two planned holidays so that we would have enough people to cover the shift, for volunteering for the paint detail on your days off, for the math project, for taking on the Academy Instructor challenge, Thank you, I noticed.

Bruce B., for coming to work in pain unable to hear when you could have easily called off, for being my straight-man in briefings and asking the questions others wanted to, for working through adversity, Thank you, I noticed.

Rosemarie P., for reminding me what I was forgetting, for giving up your slot as part of my grand plan for Layne D., for always looking out for me, Thank you, I noticed.

Kelly S., for always being willing to change your assignment, for coming in when you could have easily called off, for helping us set the record for the most people ever to change a tire in the middle of the night, Thank you, I noticed.

John W., for being my first Lead Deputy as a Deputy II new to the shift and knowing [very] well you'd take the heat for it, you did it with incredible character, Thank you, I noticed.

As a deputy sergeant and a retired Special Forces noncommissioned officer, Tim Williams could have said, "I've been a leader for more than twenty years. I know what it is to lead, even when people's lives are on the line. I'm done learning. I will rely on my experience and finish out my career, and people better just do what I say!" He could have, but he didn't. Instead, he was open to growth. He decided to continue to be a learner. And for that reason, his life, his influence, and his potential continue to expand. He lives the Law of Expansion: Growth always increases your capacity.

That quality is present in all lifelong learners. And for that reason, their capacity keeps on expanding. It's said that when Pablo Casals was ninety-five years old, a young reporter asked, "Mr. Casals, you are ninety-five and the greatest cellist that ever lived. Why do you still practice six hours a day?"

Mr. Casal's answer was telling: "Because I think I'm making progress."

You have the potential to keep making progress until the day you die—if you have the right attitude about growth. You need to believe what Rabbi Samuel M. Silver did. "The greatest of all miracles," he said, "is that we need not be tomorrow what we are today, but we can improve if we make use of the potentials implanted in us by God."

> "The greatest of all miracles," he said, "is that we need not be tomorrow what we are today, but we can improve if we make use of the potentials implanted in us by God."
>
> —Samuel M. Silver

Applying
the Law of Expansion
to Your Life

1. Have you made the mental transition from *I Can't!* or *Can I?* to *How can I?* Test yourself. Do some dreaming. Then ask yourself,

> If I knew I could not fail, what would I attempt?
> If I had no limitations, what would I like to do?
> If finances were not an issue, what would I be doing with my life?

Take time and write your answers to those questions.

Now, look at your answers. What is your gut-level response to them? Do you look at them and think, *That's far-fetched? This is impossible. How outlandish!* Or do you look at them and think, *How can I do that? What must I do to make this happen? What will I have to trade to make this transition?* If it's the latter, you are mentally ready to expand your capacity. If it's the former, you still have work to do. Spend some time figuring out what's stopping you from believing you can make the changes necessary to expand your life.

2. Give yourself an effectiveness audit so you can be sure you are thinking *What works?* instead of *more work.* Go back through your calendar and to-do lists from the past four weeks. (By the way, if you aren't using some kind of system to plan your days, that's the first step you need to take.) Try to quantify the amount of time you spent on every action and activity during those four weeks. Then think about how much time you believe each activity should have taken, and give yourself an efficiency rating from A+ to F. Now sort all the activities into categories.

> Give yourself an effectiveness audit so you can be sure you are thinking *What works?* instead of *more work.*

Where do you see patterns? What's working? What isn't working? What are you doing too much of, either because you're not being efficient enough or because the activity is off purpose? What changes do you need to make? Use the criteria of *required, return,* or *reward* to help you make judgments on what needs to change.

3. Do you have a plan and system to make sure you are doing what's important daily? First, define what is essential to you on a daily basis. In my book *Today Matters*, I wrote about my daily dozen. I include the list here for you as an idea starter:

> Choose and display the right attitudes.
> Determine and act on important priorities.
> Know and follow healthy guidelines.
> Communicate with and care for my family.
> Practice and develop good thinking.
> Make and keep proper commitments.
> Earn and properly manage finances.
> Deepen and live out my faith.
> Initiate and invest in solid relationships.
> Plan for and model generosity.
> Embrace and practice good values.
> Seek and experience improvements.

Once you've created your own list, figure out how you will manage to follow through on each of those priorities every day so you stay on track and continue to expand your potential.

15

The Law of Contribution

Growing Yourself Enables You to Grow Others

If you're not doing something with your life,
it doesn't matter how long it is!

When I started my growth journey after my conversation with Curt Kampmeier forty years ago, I had no idea where it would take me. In the beginning I only knew that I needed to grow and that I had to be intentional about it.

I must confess that in the beginning, my motivation for personal growth was selfish. I wanted to grow so I could be successful. There were goals I wanted to accomplish and milestones I wanted to achieve. But along the way, I made a life-changing discovery. My progress in personal growth also opened the doors for others. It made it possible for me to make a contribution to them. It led us not just to the achievement of success, but to work of significance. Out of what I had received in my development, I was also able to give. The confidence I gained from personal growth gave me credibility and made me believe I could start developing others. And in that, I found life's greatest joy and reward.

It is my hope that this final chapter will inspire you to be all you can be so you can help others to be all they can be. You cannot give what you do not have. But if you have worked to learn or earn something, you have the ability to pass it on to others. If you live by the Law of Contribution, you will have much to give other people, because growing yourself enables you to grow others.

Early Inspiration

Adding value to others is a high priority in my life.

> "I would rather have it said 'he lived usefully' than 'he died rich.'"
>
> —Benjamin Franklin

This desire was stirred in me as a teenager when I read about Benjamin Franklin, who once wrote, "I would rather have it said 'he lived usefully' than 'he died rich.'" More than just words, it was the way Franklin lived his life. For example, when he developed what came to be known as the Franklin stove, he could have patented it and made a good income from it. Instead, he decided to share the invention with the world.

According to Dr. John C. Van Horne of the Library Company of Philadelphia, "Franklin's philanthropy was what I call of a collective nature. His sense of benevolence was aiding his fellow human beings and doing good to society. In fact, in one sense, Franklin's philanthropy, his sense of benevolence, was his religion. Doing good to mankind was, in his understanding, divine."

Franklin didn't see the world in terms of how much he could make from it. He saw it in terms of how many people he could help. He helped develop the concepts of the lending library and local fire departments. Even his work as a printer reflects his desire to share ideas, not hoard them.

One of the things that struck me as a teen was reading that every day Franklin asked himself in the morning, "What good shall I do today?" and in the evening, "What good have I done

> Every day Ben Franklin asked himself in the morning, "What good shall I do today?" and in the evening, "What good have I done today?"

today?" That inspired me. It made me realize that I could become more intentional in my ability to help others and keep myself accountable for it on a daily basis. As I have gotten older, that has changed from being merely a good idea to becoming my greatest desire.

This became crystal clear to me when I had a heart attack in 1998. In the moments I lay there in pain, not knowing whether I would survive, I wasn't afraid of dying. I had two thoughts: The first was that I wanted to make sure the people closest to me knew how much I loved them. But the second thing I thought about was that I still had a lot I wanted to accomplish. I had contributions I still wanted to make. Fifty-one was too young to die. I later learned that David Rae of the Young Presidents' Organization says that most CEOs are less afraid of dying than they are of not making a contribution to their world, so my feelings are evidently not unusual.

> CEOs are less afraid of dying than they are of not making a contribution to their world.

Good Modeling

My desire to help others didn't come only from reading about great leaders, such as Benjamin Franklin. It was also inspired by good modeling from my parents. For years I watched my mother, who was a longtime librarian, become the chief encourager and confidante to many young women at the college where my father served as president. She made a difference in so many of their lives.

I also saw it from my father. I watched as he served the people of his congregation when he was a local church pastor. Then I saw him serve and add value to pastors when he worked as a district superintendent. And he continually added value to students and faculty alike when he led the college. And Dad's still helping others. A few years ago, Dad was getting ready to move into a new assisted-care living center, and he let me know that he wanted to be the first person to move in when it opened. "That's important, son. I need to be first," he emphasized.

Now, it's a Maxwell family trait to want to win at anything and everything, but I suspected that Dad was up to something. "Why do you want to get there first, Dad?" I asked.

"You see," he responded, "there will be a lot of old people moving into that facility"—Dad was in his late eighties at that time!—"and it's going to be foreign to them. And they're going to be scared. I want to be all moved in so I can greet them as they arrive, introduce myself, show them around, and let them know that everything will be all right."

When I grow up, I want to be more like my dad!

Be a River, Not a Reservoir

How do you increase your chances of being able to help others and make a significant contribution in your lifetime? Think of yourself as a river instead of a reservoir. Most people who do make personal growth part of their lives do it to add value to themselves. They are like reservoirs that continually take in water but only to fill themselves up. In contrast, a river *flows*. Whatever water it receives, it gives away. That's the way we should be as we learn and grow. That requires an abundance mind-set—a belief that we will keep receiving. But as long as you are dedicated to personal growth, you will never experience scarcity and will always have much to give.

Recently Margaret and I heard Gordon MacDonald speak. He challenged us to find someone who could encourage us and then to become an encouragement to others. He asked the following questions:

Who mentors you and offers a baseline of wisdom?
Who mentors you to aspire to be a better person?

Who challenges you to think?

Who cheers on your dreams?

Who cares enough to rebuke you?

Who is merciful when you have failed?

Who shares the load in pressurized moments without being asked?

Who brings fun and laughter into your life?

Who gives you perspective when you become dispirited?

Who inspires you to seek faithfully after God?

Who loves you unconditionally?

These questions are excellent for identifying someone who can encourage us to become our best. But we should also turn them around so we think about taking on a similar role with others. Whom do you mentor? Do you share the load in pressurized moments without being asked? As former president Jimmy Carter said, "I have one life and one chance to make it count for something.... My faith demands that I do whatever I can,

> "I have one life and one chance to make it count for something.... My faith demands that I do whatever I can, wherever I am, whenever I can, for as long as I can with whatever I have to try to make a difference."
>
> —*Jimmy Carter*

wherever I am, whenever I can, for as long as I can with whatever I have to try to make a difference."

Making the Right Contribution Choices

Giving of your time, expertise, and resources without expecting anything in return is an unselfish act that makes the world a better place. We need more givers. I can't explain why it works this way, but when you focus more on the wants and needs of others, more of your own wants and needs are met. In contrast, when you choose to hoard what you have, rather than give, you become the center of your own lonely universe and you become less content, not more. As a result, you repel both people and potential blessings.

You can become a more generous and giving person, even if you already exhibit those qualities. However, to do that, you must be a growing and developing person. And you must be intentional in your efforts to add value to others. Here are some suggestions to help you cultivate an attitude of contribution:

1. Be Grateful

People who aren't grateful are not givers. They rarely think about others; they think only of themselves. Their days consist of looking for others to help them, give to them, serve them. And whenever others don't fulfill those expectations, they wonder why. Their selfishness keeps them from sowing and their ingratitude makes them wonder why they don't reap a harvest!

When I was a kid, my dad helped me to understand that everybody depends on and gets help from others. He used to say, "When you were born you already owed your mother for nine months of room and board!" And after I started to pursue personal growth diligently, the concept of others helping me along the way was reinforced. In 1975 when I went to see Zig Ziglar speak for the first time, he said, "You can get everything in life you want *if* you help enough people get what they want." Those words stuck with me. And it became obvious to me that many people had helped—and still were helping—me along the way. Every author who wrote a book that I read. Every leader who took the time to teach me. Every individual who worked as a volunteer in my church. No one succeeds alone.

Many years ago I came across the following words that express this idea. I don't know who originally wrote them, but I've quoted them—and tried to live them—for forty years:

There is no success without sacrifice. If we succeed without sacrifice, then it is because someone who went before us made the sacrifice. If you sacrifice and don't see success, then someone who follows will reap success from your sacrifice.

I am the recipient of many benefits that I do not deserve and did not earn. Someone else paid for them. I am grateful! How do I show my gratitude? By daily pouring into others and passing on to them the things that will allow them to run far and achieve beyond what I have done. As you receive, I hope you will do the same.

2. Put People First

The older I've gotten, the more I've realized the importance of other people. All the things of this world are temporary. People are what matter. Your career, hobbies, and other interests will die with you. People continue on. What you give to help others builds them up enough that they are able to give to others. It's a cycle that can continue on long after you're dead and gone.

Treating others well not only benefits people, it also helps us navigate life better and puts us in a place where we can learn from others. As George Washington Carver observed, "How far you go in life depends

on your being tender with the young, compassionate with the aged, sympathetic with the striving, and
tolerant of the weak and strong. Because some day in
life you will have been all of these."

If you are a leader, putting people first is even more
important, because your actions impact so many
other people. For example, you hear it said in organizations all the time that people are their most appre-
ciable asset, yet many leaders don't behave as if that
were true. I should know: As a young leader, I erred
in thinking that my vision came first. I believed that
my most important responsibility was to get people
to buy into me, where I was going, what I was doing,
what I was asking. I thought people were supposed to
serve me for the sake of the vision. The problem with
that kind of attitude is that the line between motivating people and manipulating them is very thin and
easy to cross.

When a leader attempts to engage people, the first
question they ask is not, "Where are you going?"
Their first question is, "Do you care for me?" This
is true whenever two people want to do something
together, not just between leaders and followers. But
people especially want to know that they matter to
someone leading them and that their leader can be
trusted.

Once people are satisfied that your motives are right and that you will put them ahead of your own selfish interests, then they are willing to become partners with you in the journey. That's what they desire to be, not merely passive followers—or worse yet, expendable cogs in some sort of machine you're building.

The measure of success is not the number of people who serve you, but the number of people you serve. When people are number one in your life, adding value to them becomes natural. You do it as a matter of lifestyle. You add value to people because you value people and you believe that they have value.

> The measure of success is not the number of people who serve you, but the number of people you serve.

3. Don't Let Stuff Own You

According to my friend Earle Wilson, people can be divided into three groups: haves, have-nots, and have not paid for what they have. Unfortunately more and more people are being added to the third group every day. People are becoming enslaved to the desire to acquire. It's one of the reasons the United States and Europe are in such dire financial straits. They keep borrowing to offset their spending habit.

Author Richard Foster writes, "Owning things is

an obsession in our culture. If we own it, we feel it will give us more pleasure. The idea is an illusion." Owning things doesn't bring real satisfaction. In general, if you try to feed emotional or spiritual needs with material things, all it does is make you hungrier for more things. It doesn't satisfy. However, if you meet those needs appropriately, then you can be content with or without a lot of possessions.

No one should ever become a slave to his stuff. No one should make acquiring more just for the sake of having more his life's work. There is a story in the Bible about a man whose stuff controlled his thinking and his life. His selfishness allowed him not to see the big picture. He was consumed with gathering wealth and felt this would go on forever. However, his life was cut short and he failed to make deposits into the lives of others. Author John Ortberg writes of him,

> He devoted his life to the wrong things. If you were to make a list of his priorities, it would look something like this:
>
> **What Matters Most**
> 1. Harvest large crop
> 2. Build bigger barns
> 3. Achieve financial security

4. Eat
5. Drink
6. Be merry
7. Remember not to die

And of course, the last item is the really hard one. Sooner or later our souls will return to their Maker. And the things you have stored up—whose will they be?[1]

In 1889, millionaire industrialist Andrew Carnegie wrote an essay called "Gospel of Wealth." In it he said that the life of a wealthy person should have two periods: a time of acquiring wealth and a time of redistributing it. The only way to maintain an attitude of generosity is to make it your habit to give—your time, attention, money, and resources. Richard Foster advises, "Just the very act of letting go of money, or some other treasure, does something within us. It destroys the demon greed."

> "Just the very act of letting go of money, or some other treasure, does something within us. It destroys the demon greed."
>
> —Richard Foster

If you want to be in charge of your heart, don't allow possessions to take charge of you. The question is, "Do you own your stuff or does your stuff own you?" Contributors take the stuff they own and use it as an asset to make this world a better place to live. And they do this regardless of how much or how little they have.

4. Don't Let People Own You

When Margaret and I were newly married and I was starting my career, we had very few resources. Basically, we were scraping to get by. During that time, we became friends with a couple that was financially well off. Each Friday night, Jack and Helen would take us to a fine restaurant and buy our meal. It was the highlight of my week, since Margaret and I could not afford to eat there. Over a two-year period we received many wonderful benefits of this friendship, and we were very grateful.

After three years in that position, I got an offer to become the leader of a larger church. It was a tremendous opportunity with great advancement and potential. When I announced that I would be leaving to take it, Jack was not pleased. I'll never forget his words: "John, how can you leave after all that I have done for you?" It was in that moment that I realized Jack was starting to slowly own me. He was keeping score, and I had no idea!

It was a wake-up call. That was the day I made a choice. I would always try to give more than I received in relationships. And I would never keep score. From that day forward, I never let one of my leaders pick up the check at a restaurant. I would be on the giving side of life whenever possible. Obviously I still receive from others. I've already explained that. I am blessed beyond words for what others have done for me. But I didn't want to give away control of my life. It's hard to give yourself away when someone else owns you. I wanted to be able to value people with no strings attached. A giving life should be liberating to yourself and to those you help.

> "I consider the success of my day based on the seeds I sow, not the harvest I reap."
> —Robert Louis Stevenson

5. Define Success as Sowing, Not Reaping

Novelist Robert Louis Stevenson said, "I consider the success of my day based on the seeds I sow, not the harvest I reap." That should be the way we judge not only our days, but our entire lives. Unfortunately most people sow little and expect to reap a lot. Their focus is on payday.

Why is that? Obviously there is the issue of natural selfishness. But I think there's more to it than that. My friend Nabi Saleh, who owns Gloria Jean's Coffee, once told me, "After sowing there is a period of time when it looks like nothing is hap-

> "After sowing there is a period of time when it looks like nothing is happening. All the growth is below the surface."
> —*Nabi Saleh*

pening. All the growth is below the surface." People often don't recognize that, nor have they anticipated it and planned for it. They become impatient. And they give up.

In his book *Halftime*, Bob Buford writes about an executive who was seeking advice for how to live his life. Buford writes,

A friend of mine who had been president of a large publishing company once sought out a world-renowned Zen master. After unloading the tremendous business of his life onto the Zen master without provoking much response, he decided to be quiet for a moment. The Zen Master began to pour tea into a beautiful Oriental teacup until it overflowed the cup and spread across the grass mat toward my friend. Bewildered, my friend asked the Zen Master what he was doing. The Zen Master replied:

Your life is like a teacup, flowing over. There's no room for anything new. You need to pour out, not take more in.[2]

If you are sowing only for quick returns in life, then you will usually be unhappy with the outcome and unable to keep giving and living while waiting. On the other hand, if you sow continually and abundantly, you can be sure that in due season there will be a harvest. Successful people know this and focus on sowing, knowing that reaping will eventually come. The process is automatic. If you live life with the intention of making a difference in others' lives, your life will be full, not empty.

I love the way George Washington Carver expressed the idea. He said, "No individual has any right to come into the world and go out of it without leaving behind him distinct and legitimate reasons for having passed through it." That's something we should always keep in mind.

> "No individual has any right to come into the world and go out of it without leaving behind him distinct and legitimate reasons for having passed through it."
>
> —*George Washington Carver*

6. Focus on Self-Development, Not Self-Fulfillment

One of the more important things my mentor, consultant Fred Smith, taught me was never to focus my life on self-fulfillment. He said,

Self-fulfillment thinks of how something serves me.
Self-development thinks of how something helps me to serve others.

With self-fulfillment, feeling good is the product.
With self-development, feeling good is the by-product.

What's the main difference? The motive. Self-fulfillment means doing what I enjoy most and will receive the most strokes for doing, while self-development means doing what I am talented and uniquely fit to do, and that becomes my responsibility.

Chasing self-fulfillment is a bit like chasing happiness. It's an emotion that cannot be sustained. It relies too much on circumstances. It depends on a person's mood. In contrast, you can develop yourself regardless of how you feel, what circumstances you find yourself in, your financial situation, or the people around you.

7. Keep Growing to Keep Giving

Whenever people stop actively learning and growing, the clock has started ticking down to a time when they will no longer have anything left to give. If you want to keep giving, you have to keep growing.

> If you want to keep giving, you have to keep growing.

Sometimes people stop learning because they become complacent. They believe they have grown enough, or they want only to make the most of what they already have in terms of skill and knowledge. But when that happens, they start to plateau and then decline. They lose their innovative spirit. They begin to think about being efficient instead of breaking ground. They cut costs instead of investing in growth. Their vision becomes very limited. And instead of playing to win, they start playing not to lose.

The second thing that happens to people who stop trying to actively grow is they lose their passion. We all love doing what we're good at, but being good at something requires us to keep our skills sharp. Less skill leads to less enthusiasm and eventually discontent. If we reach this stage, we start looking behind us, because that is where our best days are. We think about the good old days, the glory days. At that point, we're only a few short steps from obsolescence. Nobody wants to learn from a has-been. What kind of contribution can we make if we get to this point? I want to give until I've given all I have. To do that I must keep growing until I can grow no more.

A Legendary Contributor

In December of 2009, a legendary personal-growth teacher, writer, and mentor died. His name was Jim Rohn. As a kid, Rohn grew up on a farm in Idaho. After graduating from high school, he went off to college but stayed for only a year. "One year of college," Rohn said, "and I thought I was thoroughly educated." Rohn took a job as a stock clerk at Sears, but he lived from paycheck to paycheck. By age twenty-five, he became discouraged. He hoped to find a better path.

A friend of Rohn's invited him to attend a seminar presented by J. Earl Shoaff, a motivational speaker and salesman. The main message: Work harder on yourself than you do on your job; your income is directly related to your philosophy, not the economy; and for things to change, you must change.[3]

Shoaff mentored Rohn for five years, encouraging

him to develop himself and pursue his dream of creating a better life for himself and his family. By age thirty-one, Rohn was a millionaire.

Rohn might have been a success story few people knew about, but then his life took an unexpected turn. A friend invited him to speak about his accomplishments at a Rotary Club meeting. Rohn accepted and gave a message that he called "Idaho Farm Boy Makes It to Beverly Hills." It was a hit. Others began to invite him to speak. At first he spoke to service organizations and to high school and college students. But he soon realized that people were hungry for what he was willing to teach. In 1963, he launched a conference business.[4]

During a career developing people that lasted more than four decades, Rohn wrote more than two dozen books, spoke at more than six thousand events, and developed around 5 million people. And during that time he never stopped learning and growing. He observed, "The greatest gift you can give to someone is your own personal development. I used to say, 'If you will take care of me, I will take care of you.' Now I say, 'I will take care of me for you if you will take care of you for me.'"

> "The greatest gift you can give to someone is your own personal development."
> —Jim Rohn

One of the greatest measures of Rohn's impact is

the number of high-profile authors and developers of people who consider him a mentor. At a tribute in his honor that was held in Anaheim, California, on February 6, 2010, guest speakers who honored him included a who's who of speakers and mentors: Anthony Robbins, Les Brown, Brian Tracy, Chris Widener, Denis Waitley, and Darren Hardy.[5]

How was Rohn able to help so many people grow? And to help so many who became well-known teachers and mentors in their own right? By continually developing himself. He understood that growing yourself enables you to grow others. He lived by the Law of Contribution.

George Bernard Shaw, the writer who won the Nobel Prize for literature in 1925, understood that the best use of a human life is in the service of others. He said,

> This is the true joy of life, the being used for a purpose recognized by yourself as a mighty one; the being a force of nature instead of a feverish, selfish little clod of ailments and grievances complaining that the world will not devote itself to making you happy. I am of the opinion that my life belongs to the whole community, and as long as I live it is my privilege to do for it whatever I can. I want to be thoroughly

used up when I die, for the harder I work the more I live. I rejoice in life for its own sake. Life is no brief candle to me. It is a sort of splendid torch which I have got hold of for the moment, and I want to make it burn as brightly as possible before handing it on to future generations.[6]

If you want to make your life burn brightly for others and future generations, keep growing.

Applying
the Law of Contribution
to Your Life

1. What is your underlying desire in life: Is it self-fulfillment or self-development? Are your efforts designed to make you feel good? Or to make you be your best? Is your goal to be successful? Or to achieve significance? Are you trying to achieve so you can feel happy? Or are you trying to put yourself in a place to help others win?

These distinctions may seem subtle, but they really make a difference. Trying to feel fulfilled is a never-ending restlessness because you will never be completely satisfied with your progress. Trying to develop yourself is a never-ending journey and will always inspire you, because every bit of progress is a victory; yet there will always be new challenges to excite and inspire you.

2. Make sure that no person owns you. Make a list of the key people in your life. Now think about each relationship and determine if you are mostly the giver, you are mostly the taker, or the relationship is even.

If you are primarily the taker, then you need to make adjustments so the other person doesn't have power over you. How do you do that? By making the effort to outgive the people in your life without keeping score. You can do this not only with your family and friends, but even with your employer. Make an effort to give more work than your organization pays you for. Not only will the people you work for and with value you, but you will add value to them. And if you have an opportunity to move on to bigger and better things, you will be able to do so knowing that you have always given your best.

3. I have one final application exercise for you in this book, and that is to put people first in your life. Write down your top three to seven goals and dreams. Now write down the names of the most important people in your life. Be honest with yourself. Which comes first? The people? Or your goals and dreams? If you are like I was early in my career, my agenda was first. Fortunately, I realized very early in my marriage that I needed to put Margaret first. That opened the door for me to be less selfish in other areas of my life. Then when my children came along, I had to put them ahead of many other things. The longer I live, the more important people have become to me. At this stage of life, nearly everything I do—

even related to personal growth—is motivated by a desire to help others.

Make the decision to put others ahead of your own agenda. Put your family ahead of your own agenda. Put the development of people at the workplace ahead of your own advancement. Serve others instead of yourself. Commit to it, and then invite others in your life to hold you accountable. And remember, sometimes the seeds you sow take a long time to grow. But you *always* see a harvest.

Notes

1. The Law of Intentionality

1. Jennifer Reed, "The Time for Action is Now!" *SUCCESS*, April 19, 2011, accessed July 11, 2011, http://www.success magazine.com/the-time-for-action-is-now/PARAMS/ article/1316/channel/22#.

2. The Law of Awareness

1. William Beecher Scoville and Brenda Milner, "Loss of Recent Memory after Bilateral Hippocampal Lesions," *Journal of Neurology, Neurosurgery, and Psychiatry*, 20 (1957), 11–21.
2. Author and source unknown.

3. The Law of the Mirror

1. Johnnetta McSwain, *Rising Above the Scars* (Atlanta: Dream Wright Publications, 2010), 14.
2. *The Road Beyond Abuse*, Georgia Public Broadcasting, accessed July 15, 2011, YouTube.com/watch ?v=iABNie9fFTk.
3. McSwain, *Rising Above the Scars*, 104–105.
4. *The Road Beyond Abuse*.
5. McSwain, *Rising Above the Scars*, 129.

6. *The Road Beyond Abuse.*
7. Ibid.
8. John Assaraf and Murray Smith, *The Answer: Grow Any Business, Achieve Financial Freedom, and Live an Extraordinary Life* (New York: Atria Books, 2008), 50.
9. Jack Canfield with Janet Switzer, *The Success Principles: How to Get from Where You Are to Where You Want to Be* (New York: Harper Paperbacks, 2006), 244–245.
10. Kevin Hall, *Aspire: Discovering Your Purpose Through the Power of Words* (New York: William Morrow, 2010), 58.

4. The Law of Reflection

1. "Re: Experience is the best teacher," *The Phrase Finder* (blog), accessed October 6, 2011, http://www.phrases.org .uk/bulletin_board/21/messages/1174 .html.

5. The Law of Consistency

1. Jack and Suzy Welch, *Winning: The Answers: Confronting 74 of the Toughest Questions in Business Today* (New York: HarperCollins, 2006), 185–186.
2. "Sunday People in Sports," *Houston Chronicle*, December 24, 2000, 15B.
3. Darren Hardy, *The Compound Effect* (Lake Dallas, TX: Success Books, 2010), 9–10.
4. "John Williams, Wikipedia, accessed August 19, 2011, http://en.wikipedia .org/wiki/John_Williams.
5. James C. McKinley Jr., "John Williams Lets His Muses Carry Him Along," *New York Times*, August 19, 2011, http://artsbeat.blogs.nytimes.com/2011/08/19/john -williams-lets-his-muses-carry-him-along/.
6. Ibid.

7. Ibid.

8. James C. McKinley Jr., "Musical Titan Honors His Heroes," *New York Times*, August 18, 2011, accessed August 19, 2011, http://www.nytimes.com/2011/08/19/arts/design/john-williams-honors-copland-bernstein-and-koussevitzky.html?_r=1.

6. The Law of Environment

1. Proverbs 13:20, NIV.

2. Wallace D. Wattles, *The Science of Getting Rich* (Holyoke, MA: Elizabeth Towne, 1910), 105.

7. The Law of Design

1. Kevin Hall, *Aspire*, 31.

2. Harvey Penick with Bud Shrake, *The Game for a Lifetime: More Lessons and Teachings* (New York: Simon and Schuster, 1996), 200.

3. Ibid, 207.

4. Harvey Penick with Bud Shrake, *Harvey Penick's Little Red Book: Lessons and Teachings from a Lifetime of Golf* (New York: Simon and Schuster, 1996), 21.

5. Ibid, 22.

8. The Law of Pain

1. "What We Know About the Health Effects of 9/11," NYC.gov, accessed October 3, 2011, http://www.nyc.gov/html/doh/wtc/html/know/mental.shtml.

2. Cheryl McGuinness with Lois Rabey, *Beauty Beyond the Ashes: Choosing Hope after Crisis* (Colorado Springs: Howard Publishing, 2004), 209.

3. Ibid, 190.

4. Ibid, 64.

5. Joey Cresta, "Cheryl McGuinness Hutchins: God Provided Strength to Overcome 9/11 Heartbreak," *Seacoast Online*, September 11, 2011, accessed October 10, 2011, http://www.seacoastonline.com/articles/20110911 -NEWS -109110324.

9. The Law of the Ladder

1. James M. Kouzes and Barry Z. Posner, *The Leadership Challenge*, 4th Edition, New York: Jossey-Bass, 2007), 28–30.

2. Ibid, 32.

3. Bill Thrall, Bruce McNicol, and Ken McElrath, *The Ascent of a Leader: How Ordinary Relationships Develop Extraordinary Character and Influence* (New York: Jossey-Bass, 1999), 17.

4. Proverbs 23:7, NIV.

5. Matthew 7:12, THE MESSAGE.

6. Welch and Welch, *Winning: The Answers*, 197.

10. The Law of the Rubber Band

1. Quoted in Craig Ruff, "Help, Please," *Dome Magazine*, July 16, 2010, accessed October 25, 2011, http://dome magazine.com/craigsgrist/cr0710.

2. Quoted in Dan Poynter, "Book Industry Statistics," Dan Poynter's ParaPublishing.com, accessed October 25, 2011, http://parapublishing.com/sites/para/resources/statistics .cfm.

3. Edmund Gaudet, "Are You Average?" *The Examiner*, January 1993, accessed January 30, 2012, http://www .theexaminer.org/volume8/number1/average.htm.

11. The Law of Trade-Offs

1. Herman Cain, *This is Herman Cain! My Journey to the White House* (New York: Threshold Editions, 2011), 45.
2. Ibid, 49–50.
3. Ibid, 50.
4. Ibid, 51.
5. Ibid, 58.
6. Genesis 25:29–34, THE MESSAGE.
7. Darren Hardy, *The Compound Effect* (Lake Dallas, TX: Success Books, 2010), 59.
8. Richard J. Leider and David A. Shapiro, *Repacking Your Bags: Lighten Your Load for the Rest of Your Life* (San Francisco: Berrett-Koehler, 2002), 29.
9. Quoted in Leo Calvin Rosten, *Leo Rosten's Treasury of Jewish Quotations* (New York: McGraw-Hill, 1988).

12. The Law of Curiosity

1. Jerry Hirshberg, *The Creative Priority: Putting Innovation to Work in your Business* (New York: Harper Business, 1998), 16.
2. Roger von Oech, *A Whack on the Side of the Head* (New York: Warner Books, 1983), 58.
3. Brian Klemmer, *The Compassionate Samurai* (Carlsbad, CA: Hay House, 2008), 157.
4. James Gleick, *Genius: The Life and Science of Richard Feynman* (New York: Vintage, 1993), 30.
5. Ibid, 36.
6. Richard P. Feynman as told to Ralph Leighton (edited by Edward Hutchings), *"Surely You're Joking, Mr. Feynman!"Adventures of a Curious Character* (New York: W.W. Norton and Company, 1985), 86.

7. Ibid, 21.
8. Ibid, 72.
9. Ibid, 317.
10. Ibid, 275.
11. Ibid, 173.
12. Ibid, 174.

13. The Law of Modeling

1. Jim Collins, "Lessons from a Student of Life," *BusinessWeek*, September 28, 2005, accessed November 21, 2011, http://www.businessweek.com/print/magazine/content/05_48/b3961007.htm?chan=gl.
2. Kevin Hall, *Aspire*, 165–166.
3. Andy Stanley, *The Next Generation Leader* (Colorado Springs: Multnomah, 2003), 104–106.

14. The Law of Expansion

1. Robert J. Kriegel and Louis Patler, *If It Ain't Broke . . . Break It!* (New York: Warner Books, 1991), 44.
2. Price Pritchett, *You²: A High-Velocity Formula for Multiplying Your Personal Effectiveness in Quantum Leaps* (Dallas: Pritchett, 2007), 16.
3. Ibid, 26.
4. Kevin Hall, *Aspire*, 114–115.

15. The Law of Contribution

1. John Ortberg, *When the Game Is Over, It All Goes Back in the Box* (Grand Rapids: Zondervan, 2007), 26.
2. Bob Buford, *Halftime: Changing Your Game Plan from Success to Significance* (Grand Rapids: Zondervan, 1994), 126.

3. Erin Casey, "Jim Rohn: The Passing of a Personal-Development Legend," *SUCCESS*, accessed December 2, 2011, http://www.successmagazine.com/jim-rohn-personal-development-legend/PARAMS/article/982#.
4. "Jim Rohn's Biography," JimRohn.com, accessed December 2, 2011, http://www.jimrohn.com/index.php?main_page=page&id=1177.
5. "Celebrating the Life and Legacy of Jim Rohn," Jim Rohn.com, accessed December 2, 2011, http://tribute.jimrohn.com/.
6. George Bernard Shaw, "Epistle Dedicatory to Arthur Bingham Walkley," *Man and Superman*, accessed May 7, 2012, Bartelby.com, http://www.bartleby.com/157/100.html.

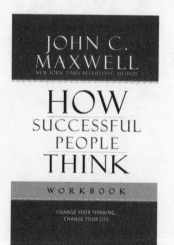

Free companion app available now for download

THE 15 INVALUABLE LAWS OF GROWTH

JOHN C. MAXWELL

Available on your iPhone and iPad, this free practical companion app will help you maximize the application of John C. Maxwell's *15 Invaluable Laws of Growth*.

- Share quotes from the book with friends via Twitter and Facebook.
- Track the progress of your personal goals.
- Create a record of your answers to key questions in the book.
- Keep important thoughts front of mind in a dedicated Favorite Quotes place.
- Sample other editions of the book and check out other John Maxwell titles.

Also look for *The 5 Levels of Leadership* App.

CENTER
STREET

THE JOHN MAXWELL COMPANY

OUR MISSION IS TO *INSPIRE,*
CHALLENGE, AND *EQUIP LEADERS*
EVERY DAY. WE SERVE OUR CLIENTS
THROUGH **EVENTS, TRAINING,**
RESOURCES AND **COACHING**.

To learn more about applying Maxwell principles to help you live out
leadership, visit **www.johnmaxwell.com** or call **1-800-333-6506**.

JESUS HAD A STRATEGY...
EQUIP LEADERS

EQUIP'S STRATEGY IS DEVELOPING
CHRISTIAN LEADERS WORLDWIDE
WITH THE SKILLS NEEDED TO
PROVIDE LEADERSHIP TO THEIR
COMMUNITIES, WORKPLACES,
AND CHURCHES.

"My vision for EQUIP is that it be continually committed to developing
leaders whose potential is great but opportunities for learning leadership
have been limited." – Founder and Chairman, John C. Maxwell

Visit **www.iequip.org** for more information.

Equipping Leaders To Reach Our World

DO YOU HAVE A PROVEN PLAN FOR
PERSONAL GROWTH?

THE JOHN MAXWELL COMPANY has developed a personal development program inspired by John C. Maxwell's latest book, *The 15 Invaluable Laws of Growth*. It is a creative and flexible system adaptable to your learning pace and style – complete with physical, virtual, and interactive components.

ARE YOU WILLING TO INVEST 5 MINUTES A DAY INTO YOUR GROWTH?

The *Maxwell Plan for Personal Growth* is based on the following core growth areas.

BET ON YOURSELF AND REACH YOUR POTENTIAL!

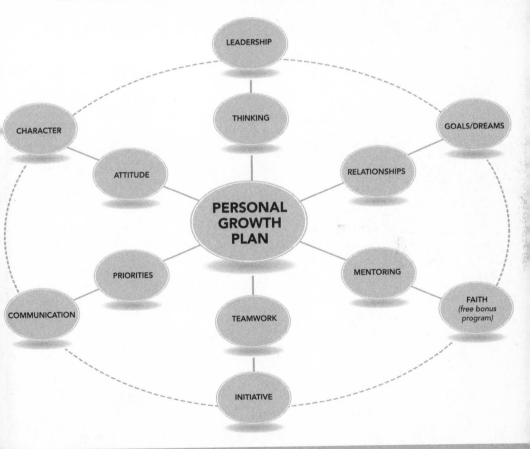